# The First

# 90

# Days

# The First
# 90
# Days

*Critical Success Strategies*
*for New Leaders at All Levels*

# Michael Watkins

Harvard Business School Press

*Boston, Massachusetts*

978-159139-110-4 (ISBN 13)

**Library of Congress Cataloging-in-Publication Data**

Watkins, Michael, 1956–
    The first 90 days : critical success strategies for new leaders at all
levels / Michael Watkins.
        p. cm.
    Includes bibliographical references and index.
    ISBN 1-59139-110-5 (alk. paper)
    1. Leadership.  2. Executive ability.  3. Strategic planning.
    4. Management.  I. Title: First ninety day.  II. Title.
    HD57.7.W38 2003
    658.4—dc21

                                            2003010766

*To Dan*

*With gratitude for your insight*
*and friendship.*

**M. W.**

# Contents

## 3. Match Strategy to Situation   59

The dangers of "one-best-way" thinking. Diagnosing the situation to develop the right strategy. The ST$_A$RS model of types of transitions. Using the model to analyze portfolios, reward success, and develop leaders.

## 4. Secure Early Wins   79

Avoiding common traps. Figuring out A-item priorities. Creating a compelling vision. Building personal credibility. Getting started on improving organizational performance. Plan-then-implement change versus collective learning.

## 5. Negotiate Success   103

Building a productive working relationship with a new boss. The five-conversations framework. Defining expectations. Agreeing on a diagnosis of the situation. Figuring out how to work together. Negotiating for resources. Putting together your 90-day plan.

## 6. Achieve Alignment   129

The role of the leader as organizational architect. Identifying the root causes of poor performance. Aligning strategy, structure, systems, skills, and culture.

## 7. Build Your Team   157

Inheriting a team and changing it. Managing the tension between short-term and long-term goals. Working team restructuring and organizational architecture issues in parallel. Putting in place new team processes.

# Preface

As long as there have been leaders, there have been leadership transitions. The changing of the guard and the challenges it poses for the new leader are as old as human society. Those challenges have not gotten any easier given the complexity of modern organizations and the speed at which business gets conducted. So if you feel that you are in over your head in your new position, you are in good company.

This book is your road map for taking charge in your first 90 days in a new job. Why do you need it? Because transitions are critical times when small differences in your actions can have disproportionate impacts on results. Leaders, regardless of their level, are most vulnerable in their first few months in a new position because they lack detailed knowledge of the challenges they will face and what it will take to succeed in meeting them; they also have not yet developed a network of relationships to sustain them. Failure to create momentum during the first few months virtually guarantees an uphill battle for the rest of your tenure in the job. Building credibility and securing some early wins lay a firm foundation for longer-term success.

The transition acceleration model presented in this book extends the work that I did with Dan Ciampa when we wrote *Right from the Start* (Boston: Harvard Business School Press, 1999). I was proud of that work, but I also came away wanting to advance it on several fronts. First, I was convinced that leaders at all levels could benefit from guidance on how to accelerate their transitions into new positions. *Right from the Start* was addressed chiefly to top executives. So although much of its advice was general, it wasn't clear which points were relevant to all transitions and which were specific to the challenges facing senior executives. I wanted to create a more flexible framework for transition acceleration, one that would help leaders at every level. At the same time, I wanted to address some important topics in more depth, such as working with the new boss, building the team, and aligning the organization's strategy, structure, systems, and skills.

In tandem with this, I wanted to delve deeper into different *types of transitions,* to help new leaders better tailor their strategies to the details of their situations. It matters a great deal, for example, whether you are leading a start-up or taking on a turnaround or inheriting a high-performing unit. Furthermore, leaders entering new organizations face different challenges from those who are promoted from within. Transition strategy thus depends on the situation.

Finally, I wanted to explore the organizational implications of systematic attention to transition acceleration. I was struck by how few companies invested in helping their precious leadership assets succeed during transitions—arguably the most critical junctures in their careers. Why did companies leave their people to sink or swim? What would it be worth to companies if managers entering critical new positions could take charge faster?

For three years, I have explored these issues by studying dozens of leadership transitions at all levels, by designing transition acceleration programs for leading companies, and by developing an online performance-support tool for new leaders. That work has culminated in the writing of this book.

If you are reading this, you likely are transitioning into a new role. This book will equip you with strategies and tools to get up to speed faster and to achieve more, sooner. You will learn how to diagnose your situation and gain clarity about its challenges and opportunities. You will assess your strengths and weaknesses and identify your greatest personal vulnerabilities in your new situation. You will gain insight into how to learn about a new organization and establish your priorities more quickly. You will learn how to diagnose and align the strategy, structure, systems, and skills of your new organization. Perhaps most important, you will get solid advice about how to manage key relationships to leverage yourself—by building teams, creating coalitions, and recruiting a supportive network of advisers and counselors. Use this book as a road map for creating your 90-day plan. If you do, you will get up to speed, and help others do so, faster than you thought possible.

*Michael Watkins*
*Boston*

# Acknowledgments

This book is dedicated to my *Right from the Start* coauthor, Dan Ciampa. It was Dan who got me interested in leadership transitions. He contributed many important ideas and vivid examples to the book we wrote together and thus to the conceptual foundation on which this book rests. Dan's deep understanding of the challenges that face managers when they enter new senior-level positions continues to enrich my thinking. Dan is a gifted counselor of leaders and a good friend.

*The First 90 Days* is also an outgrowth of my work with Johnson & Johnson. Inaki Bastarrika, formerly of J&J's Management Education and Development (MED) department, convinced me to work with this excellent company in 1999 just after the publication of *Right from the Start,* launching a rewarding research partnership. Ron Bossert, a director of MED, was instrumental in developing the J&J Transition Leadership Forum and the Business Leaders' Program for the company's new business unit leaders. Ron also introduced me to leaders whose support was crucial, including Sharon D'Agnostino, Bill Dearstyne, Mike Dormer, Colleen Goggins, Jim Lenahan, Dennis Longstreet, Bill McComb, Pat Mutchler, Christine Poon, Peter Tattle, and

Bill Weldon. Thanks also to the high-potential leaders at J&J who energetically took part in the programs I taught there.

This book is intended to complement the Leadership Transitions online performance-support tool that I developed in partnership with Harvard Business School Publishing (HBSP). The experience of creating a Web-based support tool for new leaders unquestionably helped sharpen my thinking about transition issues. Heartfelt thanks to the e-learning group at HBSP, and especially to Michelle Barton, Sarah Cummins, Ian Fanton, and Trisytn Patrick, for making that project such a pleasure to work on.

The Division of Research at the Harvard Business School funded the research that forms the foundation of this book. The support provided by research directors Teresa Amabile and Kathleen McGinn is very much appreciated. This book, and my work more broadly, would not have been possible without the encouragement provided by members of the Negotiation, Organizations, and Markets unit at HBS, especially George Baker, Max Bazerman, Nancy Beaulieu, Mal Salter, Jim Sebenius, and Michael Wheeler. Thanks too to Jack Gabarro and Linda Hill, colleagues whose ideas significantly influenced my thinking about leadership transitions.

Finally, many thanks to my faculty assistant, Mary Alice Wood; my research assistant, Usha Thakrar; and my editor, Ann Goodsell, for their help in making this book a reality.

# The First
# 90
# Days

# Introduction:
# The First 90 Days

THE PRESIDENT of the United States gets 100 days to prove himself; you get 90. The actions you take during your first three months in a new job will largely determine whether you succeed or fail. Transitions are periods of opportunity, a chance to start afresh and to make needed changes in an organization. But they are also periods of acute vulnerability, because you lack established working relationships and a detailed understanding of your new role. If you fail to build momentum during your transition, you will face an uphill battle from that point forward.

The stakes are obviously high. Failure in a new assignment can spell the end of a promising career. But making a successful transition is about more than just avoiding failure. Some leaders do derail (and when they do, their problems can almost always be traced to vicious cycles that developed in the first few months on the job). But for every leader who fails outright, there are many others who survive but do not realize their full potential. As a result, they lose opportunities to advance in their careers, and they endanger the health of their organizations.

This book is therefore as much about *transition acceleration* as it is about failure prevention. It provides a blueprint for dramatically condensing the time it will take you to get on top of the job, regardless of your level in your organization. If you succeed in this, you will free up time to concentrate on fixing problems and exploiting opportunities in your new organization. After all, your goal should be to arrive as rapidly as possible at the *breakeven point,* where you are a net contributor of value to your new organization (see "The Breakeven Point"). Every minute you save by being systematic about accelerating your transition is a minute you gain to build the business.

---

## The Breakeven Point

The *breakeven point* is the point at which new leaders have contributed as much value to their new organizations as they have consumed from it. As shown in figure I-1, new leaders are net consumers of value early on; as they learn and begin to take action, they begin to create value. From the breakeven point onward, they are (one hopes) net contributors of value to their organizations. When 210 company CEOs and presidents were asked for their best estimates of the time it takes a typical midlevel manager in their organizations to reach the breakeven point, the average of their responses was 6.2 months.[1] The purpose of transition acceleration, then, is to help new leaders reach the breakeven point earlier. What would it be worth to an organization if all its leaders in transition could reach the breakeven point one month earlier?

---

FIGURE I - 1

## The Breakeven Point

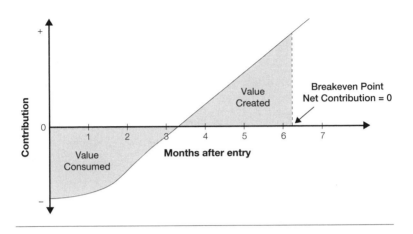

Given the stakes, it is surprising how little good guidance is available to new leaders about how to transition more effectively and efficiently into new roles. There are plenty of books and articles on leadership, but few directly address transitions at all.[2] Also, excellent resources on managing organizational change exist, but most implicitly assume the change agent is already settled in the organization, with the necessary knowledge and relationships in place to plan, build support for, and carry out transformation initiatives.

The reality is that the process of leading change often occurs in tandem with a leader's transition into a new role. This book is therefore intended to fill a gap in the leadership literature. It offers a proven blueprint for addressing the linked challenges of personal transition and organizational transformation that confront leaders in their first few months in a new job.

# Fundamental Propositions

From observing new leaders and experimenting with methods of accelerating transitions, I have developed strong beliefs about the challenges of transitions and what it takes to succeed in meeting them. These beliefs, summarized in five propositions, form the foundation of my approach to transition acceleration—and to this book.

The first proposition is that *the root causes of transition failure always lie in a pernicious interaction between the situation, with its opportunities and pitfalls, and the individual, with his or her strengths and vulnerabilities.* Failure is never just about the flaws of the new leader. Indeed, the failed leaders whom I studied had all achieved significant successes in the past. Nor is it ever just about a no-win situation in which not even a superhuman leader could have carried the day. The business situations facing leaders who derail are no tougher than those in which others succeed brilliantly. Transition failures happen when new leaders either misunderstand the essential demands of the situation or lack the skill and flexibility to adapt to them.

The second proposition is that *there are systematic methods that leaders can employ to both lessen the likelihood of failure and reach the breakeven point faster.* Early in my efforts to develop a framework for accelerating transitions at all levels, an experienced manager told me, "You can't do that." When I asked why, he said, "Because every transition is unique." This is true, of course. It is also misleading. Sure, every transition is unique if you look at its details. But viewed from a higher vantage point, we can discern types of transitions that share common features, including common traps. Consider, for example, making a transition from functional vice president to general manager. Every leader who makes this leap encounters similar challenges, such as the need to let go of reliance on functional expertise. (The transition from frontline supervisor to manager of managers represents a similar challenge at a lower level.[3]) The specific business situations that confront transitioning leaders also vary. But specific types of transition situations, such as start-ups and turnarounds, share certain features and imperatives. Further, there are fundamental principles—for example, securing early wins—that underpin success in transitions at all levels, whether one is a new supervisor or a new CEO. The key, then, is to *match your strategy to the situation.* This is a core theme to which we will return throughout the book.

The third proposition is that *the overriding goal in a transition is to build momentum by creating virtuous cycles that build credibility and by avoiding getting caught in vicious cycles that damage credibility.* Leadership is about leverage. The new leader is, after all, just one person. To be successful, she will have to mobilize the energy of many others in her organization. Her vision, her expertise, her drive can serve as a seed crystal in the new organization, one that will grow exponentially into new and more productive patterns of behavior. Too often, however, the new leader behaves more like a virus: Her early actions alienate potential supporters, undermine her credibility, and stimulate defensive reactions. As a vicious cycle takes hold, the organization's immune system gets activated and the new leader is attacked by clumps of killer cells, encapsulated, and finally expelled.

The fourth proposition is that *transitions are a crucible for leadership development and should be managed accordingly.* Precisely because they strengthen diagnostic skills, demand growth and adaptation, and test personal stamina, transitions are an indispensable development experience for every company's high-potential leaders. A survey conducted as part of McKinsey's

"War for Talent" study asked a sample of 200 senior executives to identify their five most important developmental experiences.[4] The top overall responses all involved significant transitions into new roles:

- New position with large scope

- Turning around a business

- Starting a new business

- Large, high-profile special project

- Working outside home country

This proposition emphatically does not mean—as it does at too many companies—throwing good people into the deep end to see if they sink or swim. Like swimming, transitioning is a teachable skill. Transition acceleration skills should be taught to people who are in transition, so that talented people do not drown unnecessarily.

My fifth and final proposition is that *adoption of a standard framework for accelerating transitions can yield big returns for organizations*. Each year over half a million managers enter new positions in *Fortune* 500 companies alone.[5] Given the frequency with which people take on new jobs, and the impact of each transition on others in the organization, it helps a lot if everyone—bosses, direct reports, and peers—speaks the same "transition language." Why shouldn't every person who is getting to know a new boss employ a shared set of guidelines (such as those provided in chapter 5 of this book) to build that critical relationship? Also, adopting standard approaches to learning about a new organization, securing early wins, and building coalitions translates into speedier organizational adjustments to the unavoidable stream of personnel shifts and environmental changes.

Adopting a rational framework for transition acceleration translates into real bottom-line impact.

## Accelerating Organizations

The final proposition deserves some extra emphasis and explanation. As you read what follows, think about the implications not just for you but also for your organization.

Each year slightly fewer than a quarter of the managers in a typical *Fortune* 500 company change jobs.[6] This means that managers spend an average of four years in a given position. High-potential leaders in the midsenior ranks have a shorter average time in position: Their "eras" typically last two and a half to three years. Their careers consist of a series of such eras, punctuated by transition periods of a few months during which their actions set the tone for what follows and strongly influence their overall performance.

Companies need to move their best people through positions of increasing responsibility to develop them. If they do not do so, they risk losing their best talent to competitors. But the constant churn comes at a cost. Each new manager takes time to reach the breakeven point. And the pace of business is such that there is little time available to get acclimated and little latitude for poor early decisions.

For each individual who transitions, there also are many others—direct reports, bosses, and peers—whose performance is negatively affected. In a survey of company presidents and CEOs, I asked for their best estimate of the number of people whose performance was significantly compromised by the arrival of a new midlevel manager. The average of the responses was 12.4 people.[7] In effect, all the people in the "impact network" of the transitioning manager are in transition too.

A further challenge is transitioning talented people into the organization from the outside. Even healthy organizations need to do this to introduce new ideas and preserve vitality. However, the failure rate for new leaders who enter organizations from the outside is high. Studies have found that more than 40 to 50 percent of senior outside hires fail to achieve desired results.[8] Estimates of the direct and indirect costs to a company of a failed executive-level hire range as high as $2.7 million.[9]

When surveyed, senior HR practitioners assess the challenge of coming in from the outside as "much harder" than being promoted from within.[10] They attribute the high failure rate of outside hires to several barriers to making a successful transition, notably the following:

- Executives from outside the company are not as familiar with the organizational structure and the existence of informal networks of information and communication.

- Outside hires are not familiar with the corporate culture and therefore have greater difficulty assimilating.

- New people are unknown to the organization and therefore do not have the same credibility as someone who is promoted from within.

- A long tradition of hiring from within makes it difficult for organizations to adjust to senior-level managers who are viewed as outsiders.

When a new leader fails, it is a severe, perhaps career-ending, blow to the individual. But every leadership failure—whether an outright derailment or a less dramatic underperformance— is costly for the organization as well. Success in accelerating the transitions of all managers—at every level and whether they are being promoted from within or hired from outside—could represent a tremendous gain in performance for the organization.

It is surprising, therefore, that few companies pay much attention to accelerating leadership transitions. When I lead transition acceleration programs, I ask the new leaders in the room to write down the number of transitions they have made so far in their careers and the number they anticipate making before they retire. In a group of thirty, the responses to both questions typically total more than 150 transitions! Then I ask how many participants have received training or coaching from their organization in how to make transitions, and the answer is essentially none.

All these talented people had to develop their own models for how to make transitions. This is hard-won knowledge, and the failure to share it represents a big loss for the organization. This valuable cache of experience is seldom converted into organizational learning. Also, people develop their own idiosyncratic approaches to taking charge, approaches that may or may not continue to serve them well as they rise in an organization or switch to a new one.

A shared framework for transition acceleration is therefore an organizational asset. In addition to reducing the costs of disruption, a common approach to managing leadership transitions can help you to identify and retain the best leadership talent. We don't identify star swimmers by throwing children into the pool unprepared; we teach them to swim, coach them, and then let performance speak for itself. Transition acceleration also is a skill that can be taught. Leaders should not succeed just because they happen to have mentors who are good swim coaches or because they get placed into situations that happen to play to their strengths. Neither should promising people fail because they lack these advantages. If you truly want a managerial meritocracy, then you should level the playing field during transitions.

## Success Strategies for New Leaders

Why is so little good advice available about accelerating transitions? In part, the answer is because there are many different kinds of transitions; thus, it is not enough to come up with general rules or one-size-fits-all advice. Consider the following pairs of transition situations. How do the definitions of success and the imperatives for making effective transitions differ in these cases?

- Promotion to a more senior role in marketing versus moving from marketing to a position as general manager of a business unit

- Moving to a new position within your existing organization versus moving to a new company

- Moving from a staff position to line management versus moving from line to staff

- Taking over a group facing very serious problems versus taking over a group widely and accurately viewed as very successful

The point? The challenges of transition acceleration vary depending on situational factors. It matters a great deal whether you are making a key career "passage" in terms of level in the organization, whether you are an insider or an outsider, whether you have formal authority, and whether you are taking over a successful or troubled group.[11] Thus, it is essential that you match your strategy to the situation you face.

Practical advice has to be tailored to the situation, the level of the new leader, his or her experience with the organization, and the condition of the business. That is the fundamental goal of this book: to provide new leaders with practical frameworks for diagnosing their situations and developing their own customized transition acceleration plans.

To illustrate the power of a systematic approach to transition acceleration, consider the challenge a new leader faces in diagnosing his new organization's business situation. How does he characterize the challenges and opportunities? How does he reach consensus with his new boss and direct reports about what actions need to be taken? Without a conceptual framework to guide diagnosis and planning, this turns out to be a lot of work. It is also easy to blunder into dangerous misunderstandings with bosses or direct reports about what needs doing. Even if the new leader achieves the necessary shared understanding, he is likely to have consumed significant time and energy in the process and might have missed some important opportunities and failed to identify some ticking time bombs.

Now suppose instead that the new leader is counseled to figure out early on whether his new job is a *start-up, turnaround, realignment,* or *sustaining-success* situation. Suppose too that he has clear descriptions of the challenges and opportunities typical of each of these situations and actionable guidelines for establishing priorities in each one. What changes?

This diagnostic tool, called the $ST_ARS$ model (for Start-up, Turnaround, Realignment, and Sustaining success), is developed in detail in chapter 3. It powerfully accelerates the new leader's diagnosis of his new organization and his development of effective action plans. It also helps the new leader to more rapidly reach a shared understanding of the situation with other key players, including his boss and direct reports. Whether he is taking over an entire organization or managing a group or a short-term project, he can use this tool to accelerate his transition.

So take heart. There are structural similarities in challenges and opportunities, and corresponding guidelines—must do's and don't do's—for different types of transitional situations. The key is to engage in careful diagnosis and then adapt some general principles to the demands of the situation.

## Plan of the Book

The rest of the book provides a road map for creating your 90-day acceleration plan. The conceptual backbone of the road map is ten key transition challenges:

1. **Promote yourself.** This doesn't mean hiring your own publicist. It means making the mental break from your old job and preparing to take charge in the new one. Perhaps the biggest pitfall you face is assuming that what has made you successful to this point in your career will continue to do so. The dangers of sticking with what you know, working extremely hard at doing it, and failing miserably are very real.

2. **Accelerate your learning.** You need to climb the learning curve as fast as you can in your new organization. This means understanding its markets, products, technologies, systems, and structures, as well as its culture and politics. Getting acquainted with a new organization can feel like drinking from a fire hose. You have to be systematic and focused about deciding what you need to learn and how you will learn it most efficiently.

3. **Match strategy to situation.** There are no universal rules for success in transitions. You need to diagnose the business situation accurately and clarify its challenges and opportunities. Start-ups, for instance—of a new product, process, plant, or a completely new business—share challenges quite different from those you would face while turning around a product, process, or plant in serious trouble. A clear diagnosis of the situation is an essential prerequisite for developing your action plan.

4. **Secure early wins.** Early wins build your credibility and create momentum. They create virtuous cycles that leverage the energy you are putting into the organization to create a pervasive sense that good things are happening. In the first few weeks, you need to identify opportunities to build personal credibility. In the first 90 days, you need to identify ways to create value, improve business results, and get to the breakeven point more rapidly.

5. **Negotiate success.** Because no other single relationship is more important, you need to figure out how to build a productive working relationship with your new boss and manage his or her expectations. This means carefully planning for a series of critical conversations about the situation, expectations, style, resources, and your personal development. Crucially, it means developing and gaining consensus on your 90-day plan.

6. **Achieve alignment.** The higher you rise in an organization, the more you have to play the role of organizational architect. This means figuring out whether the

organization's strategy is sound, bringing its structure into alignment with its strategy, and developing the systems and skill bases necessary to realize strategic intent.

7. **Build your team.** If you are inheriting a team, you will need to evaluate its members and perhaps restructure it to better meet the demands of the situation. Your willingness to make tough early personnel calls and your capacity to select the right people for the right positions are among the most important drivers of success during your transition. You will need to be both systematic and strategic in approaching the team-building challenge.

8. **Create coalitions.** Your success will depend on your ability to influence people outside your direct line of control. Supportive alliances, both internal and external, will be necessary to achieve your goals. You should therefore start right away to identify those whose support is essential for your success, and to figure out how to line them up on your side.

9. **Keep your balance.** In the personal and professional tumult of a transition, you will have to work hard to maintain your equilibrium and preserve your ability to make good judgments. The risks of losing perspective, getting isolated, and making bad calls are ever present during transitions. There is much you can do to accelerate your personal transition and to gain more control over your work environment. The right advice-and-counsel network is an indispensable resource.

10. **Expedite everyone.** Finally, you need to help everyone in your organization—direct reports, bosses, and

peers—accelerate their own transitions. The quicker
you can get your new direct reports up to speed, the
more you will help your own performance. Beyond
that, the benefits to the organization of systematically
accelerating everyone's transitions are potentially vast.

If you succeed in meeting these core challenges, you will have a
successful transition. Failure to surmount any one of them,
however, is enough to cause potentially crippling problems.

The chapters that follow offer actionable guidelines and tools
for succeeding in meeting each of these ten challenges. You will
learn how to diagnose your situation and create action plans tailored to your needs, regardless of your level in the organization
or the business situation you face. In the process you will build a
90-day plan that will accelerate you into your new role.

This book is for new leaders at all levels, from first-time managers to CEOs. The fundamental principles of effective transition acceleration hold up well across all levels. But the specifics
of who, what, when, and how and the relative weights of the ten
key challenges vary a lot. For more senior people, aligning the
architecture of the organization, building the team, and creating coalitions loom large. For less senior people, building a
relationship with the new boss and creating a supportive advice-
and-counsel network will be priorities. Every new leader needs
to quickly become familiar with the new organization, to secure
early wins, and to build supportive coalitions. That's why this
book provides guidelines for translating principles into plans
tailored to your own situation. As you continue through it, you
should read actively, making notes about the applicability of
specific points to your situation, as well as thinking about how
the advice should be customized to your situation.

# 1

# Promote Yourself

A FTER EIGHT YEARS in marketing at a Texas-based consumer electronics company, Julia Gould was promoted to her first project leader position. Up to that point, her track record had been stellar. Her intelligence, focus, and determination had won her recognition and early promotion to increasingly senior positions. The company had designated her a high-potential leader and had positioned her on the fast track to more senior leadership.

Julia was assigned to be the launch manager for one of the company's hottest new products. It was her responsibility to coordinate the work of a cross-functional team drawn from marketing, sales, R&D, and manufacturing. The goal: to seamlessly move the product from R&D to production, oversee a rapid ramp-up, and streamline the market introduction.

Julia ran into trouble early on. Her success in marketing was due to her extraordinary attention to detail. Accustomed to managing with authority and making the calls, she had a high need for control and a tendency to micromanage. When she tried to continue making the calls, members of the team initially said nothing. But soon two key members challenged her knowledge and authority. Stung, she focused more on the area she knew best: the marketing aspects of the launch. Her efforts to micromanage the marketing members of the team alienated them. Within a month and a half, Julia was back in marketing and someone else was leading the team.

Julia Gould failed because she was unable to make the leap from being a strong functional performer to taking on a cross-functional, project management role. She failed to grasp that the strengths that had made her successful in marketing could be liabilities in a role that required her to lead without direct authority or superior expertise. She kept doing what she knew how to do, which made her feel confident and in control. The result, of course, was the opposite. By not letting go of the past and fully embracing her new role, she squandered a big opportunity to rise in the organization.

What might Julia Gould have done differently? She should have focused on mentally promoting herself into the new position, a fundamental challenge for new leaders. "Promoting yourself" does not mean self-serving grandstanding or hiring a PR firm. It means preparing yourself mentally to move into your new role by letting go of the past and embracing the imperatives of the new situation to give yourself a running start. This can be hard work, but it is essential that you do it. All too often, promising managers get promoted but fail to promote themselves by undertaking the necessary change in perspective.

A related mistake is to believe that you will be successful in your new job by continuing to do what you did in your previous job, only more so. "They put me in the job because of my skills and accomplishments," the reasoning goes. "So that must be what they expect me to do here." This thinking is destructive because doing what you know how to do and avoiding what you don't can appear to work, at least for a while. You can exist in a state of denial, believing that because you are being productive and efficient, you are being effective. You may keep on believing this until the moment the walls come crashing down around you.

No one is immune to this trap, not even accomplished senior executives. Consider the experience of Douglas Ivester at Coca-Cola. Ivester was promoted to CEO in 1997 after the sudden death of his predecessor, the highly praised Roberto Goizueta, who had led Coke since 1981.[1] In 1999, after a string of missteps that had eroded the confidence of Coke's board of directors, Ivester resigned.

To outside observers, Ivester had appeared to be the perfect candidate for the job. "The real challenge [for Coca-Cola]," wrote one PaineWebber analyst, "is not becoming a casualty of their own success. And I think with the current lineup at Coke, starting with Doug Ivester, they're not too likely to become complacent."[2] *Fortune* dubbed him the "prototype boss for the 21st century."[3]

An accountant by training, Ivester had spent nearly twenty years rising through the ranks to become Coke's COO and Goizueta's right-hand man. Named Coke's CFO in 1985, at age thirty-seven, he quickly made his mark by orchestrating the successful 1986 spin-off of the company's bottling operations, Coca-Cola Enterprises. He also succeeded as president of European operations, his first operating role, and oversaw the company's expansion into Eastern Europe in 1989. Ivester was named president of Coke USA one year later and became president and COO of the company in 1994.

But Ivester was unable to make the leap from COO to CEO. He refused to name a new COO, even when strongly pressed to do so by Coke's board of directors. Instead, he continued to act as a "super-COO" and maintained daily contact with the sixteen people who reported to him. His extraordinary attention to detail, which had been such a virtue in finance and operations, proved to be a hindrance in this new position. Ivester could not free himself from day-to-day operations enough to take on the strategic, visionary, and statesmanlike roles of an effective CEO.

The result was a series of missteps, none fatal on its own, that cumulatively sapped Ivester's credibility. His ham-handed treatment of European regulators contributed to Coke's failure to acquire Orangina in France and drastically reduced the value of its acquisition of Cadbury Schweppes's brands. He was also widely seen as having mishandled a crisis in 1999 involving contamination of Coke bottled in Belgium by not visibly taking charge. He alienated other potential allies by failing to respond effectively to a festering racial discrimination suit in Coke's Atlanta headquarters, and by applying too much pressure to Coke's already stretched bottlers regarding concentrate pricing and inventories. By the end, Ivester had few friends.

Suggesting that Ivester's failure was the result of a fatal character flaw, the *Wall Street Journal* mused, "The job of running a giant company like Coca-Cola Co. is akin to conducting an orchestra, but M. Douglas Ivester, it seems, had a tin ear. . . . [He] knew the math, but not the music required to run the world's leading marketing organization."[4]

The root causes of Ivester's failure, however, lay less in what he could not do (or learn to do) than in what he could not let go of. An impressive career came to a deeply disappointing, even tragic, conclusion because he persisted in concentrating on what he felt most competent doing. Was his failure inevitable? Probably not. Was it likely given his approach to the transition from COO to CEO? Absolutely.

## Promoting Yourself

How can you avoid this trap? How can you be sure to embrace the challenges of your new position? This section provides some basic principles for mentally getting ready for your new position.

### Establish a Clear Breakpoint

The move from one position to another usually happens in a blur. You rarely get much notice before being thrust into a new job. A lucky new leader gets a couple of weeks, but more often the move is measured in days. You get caught up in a scramble to finish up in your old job even as you try to wrap your arms around the new one. Even worse, you may be pressured to perform both jobs until your previous position is filled, making the line of demarcation even fuzzier.

Because you may not get a clean transition in terms of job responsibilities, it is essential to discipline yourself to make the transition mentally. Pick a specific time, such as a weekend, and use it to imagine yourself being promoted. Consciously think of letting go of the old job and embracing the new one. Think hard about the differences between the two and in what ways you have to think and act differently. Take the time to celebrate your move, even informally, with family and friends. Use the time to touch base with your informal advisers and counselors and to ask for some quick advice. The bottom line: Do whatever it takes to get into the transition state of mind.

### Hit the Ground Running

Your transition begins the moment you learn you are being considered for a new job (see figure 1-1). It ends roughly 90 days after you begin the job. By this point, key people in the organization—your bosses, peers, and direct reports—expect you to be getting some traction.

A three-month time frame is not a hard and fast rule; it depends on what type of situation you are entering. Regardless, you should use the 90-day mark as a key milestone for planning purposes. It will help you confront the need to operate in a compressed time frame. If you are lucky, you may get a month or more of lead time between learning you are being considered and sitting in the chair. Use that time to begin educating yourself about your organization.

Regardless of how much preparation time you get, start planning what you hope to accomplish by specific milestones. You probably won't have much time, but even a few hours of pre-entry planning go a long way. Begin by thinking about your first day in the new job. What do you want to do by the end of that day? Then move to the first week. Then focus on the end of the first month, the second month, and finally the three-month mark. These plans will be sketchy, but the simple act of beginning to plan will help clear your head.

### Assess Your Vulnerabilities

You have been offered your new position because those who hired you think you have the skills to succeed. You probably do.

FIGURE 1 - 1

## Key Transition Milestones

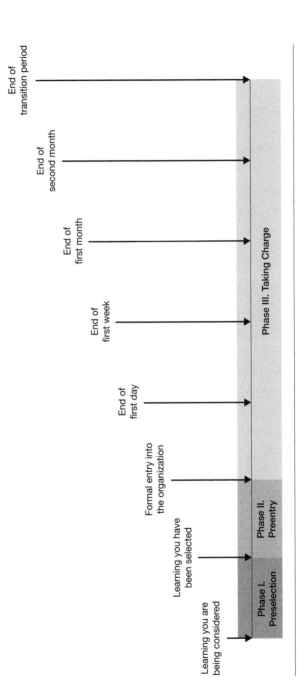

But as we saw in the cases of Julia Gould and Douglas Ivester, it can be fatal to rely too much on what made you successful in the past. As one senior executive expressed it, "Everyone has an urge to work at one level below where they are. You need to work where you are, not where you were."

One way to pinpoint your vulnerabilities is to assess your *problem preferences*—the kinds of problems toward which you naturally gravitate. Everyone likes to do some things more than others. Julia Gould's preference was marketing; for Douglas Ivester it was finance and operations. Your preferences have probably influenced you to choose jobs where you can do more of what you like to do. As a result, you perfect those skills and feel most competent when you solve problems in those areas, which reinforces the cycle. This pattern is like exercising your right arm and ignoring your left: The strong arm gets stronger and the weak one atrophies. The risk, of course, is that you create an imbalance that leaves you vulnerable in situations in which success depends on being ambidextrous.

Table 1-1 is a simple tool for assessing your preferences for different kinds of business problems. Fill in each cell by assessing your intrinsic interest in *solving problems* in the domain in question. In the first cell, for example, ask yourself how much you like to work on appraisal and reward systems. This isn't a comparative question; don't compare this interest with others. Rank your interest in each type of problem separately, on a scale of 1 (not at all) to 10 (very much). Keep in mind that you are being asked about your intrinsic *interests,* not your skills or experience. Do not turn the page before completing the table.

TABLE 1-1

## Assessment of Problem Preferences

*Assess your intrinsic interest in solving problems in each of these domains on a scale of 1 to 10, where 1 means very little interest and 10 means a great deal of interest.*

| Design of appraisal and reward systems | Employee morale | Equity/Fairness |
|---|---|---|
| _____ | _____ | _____ |
| Management of financial risk | Budgeting | Cost-consciousness |
| _____ | _____ | _____ |
| Product positioning | Relationships with customers | Organizational customer focus |
| _____ | _____ | _____ |
| Product or service quality | Relationships with distributors and suppliers | Continuous improvement |
| _____ | _____ | _____ |
| Project management systems | Relationships among R&D, marketing, and operations | Cross-functional cooperation |
| _____ | _____ | _____ |

Now transfer your rankings from table 1-1 to the corresponding cells in table 1-2. Then sum the three columns and the five rows.

The column totals represent your preferences among technical, political, and cultural problems. *Technical* problems encompass strategies, markets, technologies, and processes. *Political* problems concern power and politics in the organization. *Cultural* problems involve values, norms, and guiding assumptions.

If one column total is noticeably lower than the others, it represents a potential blind spot for you. If you score high on technical and low on cultural or political, for example, you may be at risk of overlooking the human side of the organizational equation.

The row totals represent your preferences for different business functions. A low score in any row suggests that you prefer

**TABLE 1-2**

## Preferences for Problems and Functions

|  | Technical | Political | Cultural | *Total* |
|---|---|---|---|---|
| **Human Resources** |  |  |  |  |
| **Finance** |  |  |  |  |
| **Marketing** |  |  |  |  |
| **Operations** |  |  |  |  |
| **Research and Development** |  |  |  |  |
| *Total* |  |  |  |  |

not to grapple with problems in that functional area. Again, these are potential blind spots.

The results of this diagnostic exercise should help you answer the following questions: In what spheres do you most enjoy solving problems? In what spheres are you *least* eager to solve problems? What are the implications for potential vulnerabilities in your new position?

You can do a lot to compensate for your vulnerabilities. Three basic tools are *self-discipline, team building*, and *advice and counsel.* You will need to discipline yourself to devote time to critical activities that you do not enjoy and that may not come naturally. Beyond that, actively search out people in your organization whose skills are sharp in these areas, so they can backstop you and so you can learn from them. A network of advisers and counselors can also help you move beyond your comfort zone. These strategies for compensating for your weaknesses are discussed in detail in chapter 7, "Build Your Team," and chapter 9, "Keep Your Balance."

### Watch Out for Your Strengths

Your weaknesses can make you vulnerable, but so can your strengths. Every strength has its attendant pitfalls. The qualities that have made you successful so far can prove to be weaknesses in your new role. Both Julia Gould and Douglas Ivester were attentive to detail. Though clearly a strength, attention to detail has a downside, especially in tandem with a high need for control: The result may be a tendency to micromanage people in the areas you know best. This behavior pattern can demoralize people who want to make their own contributions without intrusive oversight.

### Relearn How to Learn

It may have been a long time since you faced such a steep learning curve. "Suddenly I realized how much I didn't know" is a common lament from leaders in transition. You may have excelled in a function or discipline, like Julia Gould, and now find yourself in a general-management position. Or having flourished in line positions, you may have been called on to manage in a staff position or a matrix management arrangement. Or you may be joining a new company where you lack an established network and sense of the culture. Regardless, you suddenly need to learn a lot fast.

Having to start learning again can evoke long-buried and unnerving feelings of incompetence and vulnerability, especially if you suffer any early setbacks. You may find yourself mentally revisiting a juncture in your career when you had less confidence. Perhaps you will make some early missteps and experience failure for the first time in ages. So you unconsciously begin to gravitate toward areas where you feel competent and people who reinforce your feelings of self-worth.

New challenges and associated fears of incompetence can set up a vicious cycle of denial and defensiveness, as Chris Argyris noted in "Teaching Smart People How to Learn" in the *Harvard Business Review:*

> Because many professionals are almost always successful at what they do, they rarely experience failure. And because they have rarely failed, they have never learned how to learn from failure. So whenever their . . . learning strategies go wrong, they become defensive, screen out criticism, and put the "blame" on anyone and everyone but themselves. In short, their ability to

learn shuts down precisely at the moment they need it
the most.[5]

Put bluntly, you can decide to learn or you can become brittle
and fail. Your failure may be dramatic, like Julia Gould's, or it
may be death by a thousand cuts, as in the case of Douglas
Ivester, but it is inevitable. As we discuss in the next chapter,
denial and defensiveness are a sure recipe for disaster.

Relearning to learn can be painful. Transitioning into a new
job may revive some deep fears about your capabilities that you
thought you had long laid to rest. So if you find yourself waking
up in a cold sweat, take comfort. Most new leaders experience
the same feelings. And if you embrace the need to learn, you
can surmount them.

**Rework Your Network**

As you advance in your career, the advice and counsel you
need changes. Promoting yourself calls for working proactively
to restructure your advice-and-counsel network. Early in your
career, there is a premium on cultivating good technical advisers—experts in certain aspects of marketing or finance, for
instance, who can help you get your work done. As you are progressively promoted, however, it becomes increasingly important to get good political counsel and personal advice. Political
counselors help you understand the politics of the organization, which is especially important when you plan to implement
change. Personal advisers help you keep perspective and equilibrium in times of stress. As discussed in chapter 9, transform-
ing your advice-and-counsel network is never easy. Your current
advisers may be close friends, and you may feel comfortable
with technical advisers whose domains you know well.

### Watch Out for People Who Want
### to Hold You Back

Consciously or not, some individuals may not want you to advance. Your old boss may not want to let you go, for example. So you have to negotiate clear expectations, as soon as you know when you will be transitioning, about what you will do to close things out. This means being specific about what issues or projects will be dealt with and to what extent and, critically, what is *not* going to be done. Take notes and circulate them back to the boss, so that everyone is on the same page. Then hold your boss, and yourself, to the agreement. Be realistic about what you can accomplish. There is always more that you could do, so keep in mind that time to learn and plan before you enter a new job is a very precious commodity.

Friends may not want their relationships with you to change. But change they must, and the sooner you accept that (and help others to accept it too), the better. Others in your organization will be looking for signs of favoritism and will judge you accordingly.

If you have been promoted to supervise people who were once your peers, some may be jealous. Some may even work to undermine you. This may subside with time. But expect early tests of your authority and plan to meet them by being firm and fair. If you don't establish limits early, you will live to regret it. Getting others to accept your promotion is an essential part of promoting yourself. So if you conclude the people in question are never going to accept the situation, then you have to find a way to move them out of your organization as quickly as possible.

# Overcoming the Barriers

Promoting yourself turns out to be hard work, and some of the barriers may lie within you. Take a few minutes to think hard about your personal vulnerabilities in your new position, as revealed by your analysis of your problem preferences. How will you compensate for them? Then think about the external forces, such as commitments to your current boss, that could hold you back. How can you avoid that outcome?

To borrow an old saw, promoting yourself is a journey and not a destination. You will have to work constantly to ensure that you are engaging with the *real* challenges of your new position and not practicing what Ron Heifetz terms "work avoidance."[6] It is easy to backslide into habits that are both comfortable and dangerous. Plan to reread this chapter and its questions periodically, asking, "Am I doing all that I can to promote myself?"

## ACCELERATION CHECKLIST

*Lists like this one appear at the end of each chapter to help you crystallize the key lessons and apply them to your situation. Use these questions to guide your analysis and tailor your 90-day acceleration plan.*

1. What has made you successful so far in your career? Can you succeed in your new position by relying solely on those strengths? If not, what are the critical skills you need to develop?

2. Are there aspects of your new job that are critical to success but that you prefer not to focus on? Why is that

the case? How will you compensate for your potential blind spots?

3. What do you need to do to ensure that you make the mental leap into the new position? From whom might you seek advice and counsel on this? What other activities might help you do this?

# 2

# Accelerate
# Your Learning

CHRIS BAGLEY headed the quality function at Sigma Corporation, a medium-sized durable goods company. When Chris's boss left to become vice president of manufacturing at White Goods, a struggling manufacturer of appliances, he offered Chris a job as general manager of its largest plant. Chris jumped at the opportunity.

Sigma had built a strong manufacturing organization. Chris had joined the company right out of engineering school and rotated through most of the major manufacturing functions. He was highly skilled; however, he had grown accustomed to dealing with state-of-the-art technology and a motivated workforce. He had toured the White Goods plant before taking the job and knew that it did not come close to measuring up. He was determined to change that—and quickly.

Soon after arriving at the plant, Chris declared it outdated and went on record as saying that it needed to be rebuilt from the ground up "the Sigma way." He immediately brought in high-powered operations consultants. The consultants delivered a scathing report, characterizing the plant's technology and systems as "antiquated" and the workforce's skills as "marginal." They recommended a thorough team-based reorganization of the plant, as well as substantial investments in technology and worker training. Chris shared this report with his direct reports, saying that he planned to act quickly on the recommendations. He interpreted their silence as agreement.

Soon after the new team structure was put in place in one of the plant's four production lines, productivity plummeted and quality suffered. Chris convened his team and urged them to "get the problems fixed, and fast." But the problems remained and worker morale throughout the plant slumped.

After three months, Chris's boss told him, "You've alienated just about everyone. I brought you here to improve the plant, not tear it down." His boss then peppered him with questions: "How much time did you spend learning about this plant? Did you know they had already experimented unsuccessfully with team production? Have you seen what they were able to accomplish before you arrived with the resources they were given? You've got to stop doing and start listening."

Shaken, Chris held sobering discussions with his managers, supervisors, and groups of workers. He learned a lot about the creativity they had displayed in dealing with lack of investment in the plant. He then called a plantwide meeting and praised the workforce for doing so much before he took charge. He announced the reorganization was on hold and that they would focus on upgrading the plant's technology before making any other changes.

What did Chris do wrong? Like too many new leaders, he failed to learn enough about his new organization and so made some costly assumptions. It is essential to figure out what you need to know about your new organization and then to learn it as rapidly as you can. Why? Because efficient and effective learning reduces your window of vulnerability: You can identify potential problems that might erupt and take you off track. It also equips you to begin to make *good* business decisions earlier. Remember, your internal and external customers won't wait for you to take a leisurely stroll up the learning curve.

## Overcoming Learning Disabilities

When a new leader derails, failure to learn is almost always a factor. Information overload can obscure the most telling issues. There is so much to absorb that it is difficult to know where to focus. Amid the torrent of information coming your way, it is easy to miss important signals. Or you might focus too much on the technical side of the business—products, customers, technologies, and strategies—and shortchange the critical learning about culture and politics.

To compound this problem, surprisingly few managers have received any training in systematically diagnosing an organization. Those who have had such training invariably prove to be either human resources professionals or former management consultants.

A related problem is failure to plan to learn. Planning to learn means figuring out in advance what the important questions are and how you can best answer them. Few new leaders take the time to think systematically about their learning priorities. Fewer still explicitly create a learning plan when entering a new role.

Some leaders even have "learning disabilities," potentially crippling internal blocks to learning. One is a simple failure even to try to understand the history of the organization. A baseline question that every new leader should ask is, "How did we get to this point?" Otherwise, you risk tearing down fences without knowing why they were put up. Armed with insight into the history, you may indeed find the fence is not needed and must go. Or you may find there is a good reason to leave it where it is.

Other new leaders suffer from the action imperative, a learning disability whose primary symptom is a near-compulsive need to take action. If you habitually find yourself too anxious or too busy to devote time to systematic learning, you may suffer from this malady. It is a serious affliction, because being too busy to learn often results in a death spiral. If you do not learn, you can easily make poor early decisions that undermine your credibility, making people less likely to share important information with you, leading to more bad decisions. The result is a vicious cycle that can irreparably damage your credibility. So beware! It may feel right to enter a new situation and begin acting decisively—and sometimes, as we will see in the next chapter, it *is* the right thing to do—but you risk being poorly prepared to see the real problems.

Perhaps most destructive of all, some new leaders arrive with "the answer." They have already made up their minds about how to solve the organization's problems. Having matured in an organization where "things were done the right way," they fail to realize that what works well in one organizational culture may fail miserably in another. As Chris Bagley found out the hard way, this stance leaves you vulnerable to serious mistakes and is likely to alienate people. Bagley thought he could simply import what he had learned at Sigma to fix the plant's problems. Even in situations (such as turnarounds) in which you have been brought in explicitly to import new ways of doing things, you still have to learn about the organization's culture and politics to customize your approach. Besides, displaying a genuine ability to listen often translates into increased credibility and influence.

## Managing Learning as an Investment Process

If you approach your efforts to get up to speed as an investment process—and your scarce time and energy as resources that deserve careful management—you will realize returns in the form of actionable insights. An *actionable insight* is knowledge that enables you to make better decisions earlier and so helps you reach the breakeven point in terms of personal value creation sooner. Chris Bagley would have acted differently if he had known that (1) senior management at White Goods had systematically underinvested in the plant, despite energetic efforts by local managers to upgrade, (2) the plant had achieved remarkable results in quality and productivity given what they had to work with, and (3) the supervisors and workforce were justifiably proud of what they had accomplished.

To maximize your return on investment in learning, you have to effectively and efficiently extract actionable insights from the mass of information available to you. *Effective* learning calls for figuring out *what* you need to learn so you can focus your efforts. Devote some time to defining your learning agenda as early as possible, and return to it periodically to refine and supplement it. *Efficient* learning means identifying the best available sources of insight and then figuring out how to extract maximum insight with the least possible outlay of your precious time. Chris Bagley's approach to learning about the White Goods plant was neither effective nor efficient.

## Defining Your Learning Agenda

If Chris Bagley had it to do over, what might he have done? He would have planned to engage in a systematic learning process—creating a virtuous cycle of information gathering, analyzing, hypothesizing, and testing.

The starting point is to begin to define your learning agenda, ideally before you even formally enter the organization. A learning agenda crystallizes your learning priorities: What do you most need to learn? It consists of a focused set of questions to guide your inquiry, or hypotheses that you want to explore and test, or both. Of course, learning during a transition is iterative: At first your learning agenda will consist mostly of questions, but as you learn more you will hypothesize about what is going on and why. Increasingly, your learning will shift toward fleshing out and testing those hypotheses.

How should you compile your early list of guiding questions? Start by generating questions about the *past,* questions about the *present,* and questions about the *future.* Why are things done they way they are? Are the reasons why something was done (for example, to meet a competitive threat) still valid today? Are conditions changing such that something different should be done in the future? The accompanying boxes offer sample questions in these three categories.

## Identifying the Best Sources of Insight

You will learn from various types of hard data, such as financial and operating reports, strategic and functional plans, employee surveys, press accounts, and industry reports. But to make effective decisions, you also need "soft" information about

## Questions About the Past

### Performance

- How has this organization performed in the past? How do people in the organization think it has performed?
- How were goals set? Were they insufficiently or overly ambitious?
- Were internal or external benchmarks used?
- What measures were employed? What behaviors did they encourage and discourage?
- What happened if goals were not met?

### Root Causes

- If performance has been good, why has that been the case?
- What have been the relative contributions of the organization's strategy, its structure, its technical capabilities, its culture, and its politics?
- If performance has been poor, why has that been the case? Do the primary issues reside in the organization's strategy? Its structure? Its technical capabilities? Its culture? Its politics?

### History of Change

- What efforts have been made to change the organization? What happened?
- Who has been instrumental in shaping this organization?

## Questions About the Present

### Vision and Strategy

- What is the stated vision and strategy of the organization?
- Is it really pursuing that strategy? If not, why not? If so, is the strategy going to take the organization where it needs to go?

### People

- Who is capable and who is not?
- Who can be trusted and who cannot?
- Who has influence and why?

### Processes

- What are the key processes of the organization?
- Are they performing acceptably in terms of quality, reliability, and timeliness? If not, why not?

### Land Mines

- What lurking surprises could detonate and push you off track?
- What potentially damaging cultural or political missteps must you avoid making?

### Early Wins

- In what areas (people, relationships, processes, or products) can you achieve some early wins?

**Questions About the Future**

Challenges and Opportunities

- In what areas is the business most likely to face stiff challenges in the coming year? What can be done now to prepare for them?
- What are the most promising unexploited opportunities? What would need to happen to realize their potential?

Barriers and Resources

- What are the most formidable barriers to making needed changes? Are they technical? Cultural? Political?
- Are there islands of excellence or other high-quality resources that you can leverage?
- What new capabilities need to be developed or acquired?

Culture

- Which elements of the culture should be preserved?
- Which elements need to change?

---

the organization's strategy, technical capabilities, culture, and politics. The only way to gain this intelligence is to talk to people who have critical knowledge about your situation.

Who can provide the best return on your learning investment? Identifying promising sources will make your learning process both more complete and more efficient. Keep in mind that you need to listen to key people both *inside* and *outside* the

FIGURE 2 - 1

## Sources of Knowledge

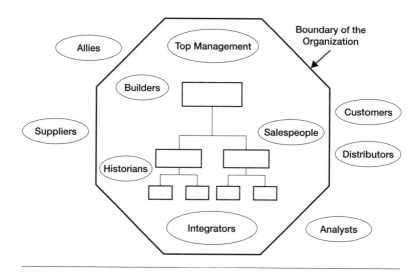

organization (see figure 2-1). Talking to people with different points of view will deepen your insight. Specifically, this will enable you to translate between external realities and internal perceptions, and between the top of the hierarchy and the people on the front lines.

The most valuable external sources of information are likely to be the following:

- **Customers.** How do customers perceive your organization? How do your best customers assess your products or services? How about your customer service? How do they rank your company against your competitors?

- **Distributors.** From distributors, you can learn about the logistics of product movement, customer service, and competitors' practices and offerings. You can also get a sense of the distributors' own capabilities.

- **Suppliers.** Suppliers can give you their perspectives on your organization in its role as a customer. You can also learn about the strengths and flaws of internal operations management and systems.

- **Outside analysts.** Analysts can give you a fairly objective assessment of your company's strategy and capabilities, as well as those of your competitors. Analysts also have a broad overview of the demands of the market and the economic health of the industry.

Indispensable internal information sources are the following:

- **Frontline R&D and operations.** These are the people who develop and manufacture your products or deliver your services. Frontline people can familiarize you with the organization's basic processes and its relationships with key external constituencies. They can also shed light on how the rest of the organization supports or undermines efforts on the front line.

- **Sales and purchasing.** These people, and customer service representatives and purchasing staff, interact directly with customers, distributors, and suppliers. Often they have up-to-date information about trends and imminent changes in the market.

- **Staff.** Talk with heads or key staff members of the finance, legal, and human resources functional areas. These people have specialized but useful perspectives on the internal workings of the organization.

- **Integrators.** Integrators are people who coordinate or facilitate cross-functional interaction, including project managers, plant managers, and product managers. You can learn from them how links within the organization work and how the functions mesh. These people can help you discover the true political hierarchies and identify where internal conflicts lie.

- **Natural historians.** Keep an eye out for "old-timers" or natural historians—people who have been with the company for a long time and those who naturally absorb the organization's history. From this group, you can learn about the company's mythology and the roots of its culture and politics.

## Adopting Structured Learning Methods

Once you have a rough sense of what you need to learn and where to seek it—whether from reports or from conversations with knowledgeable people—the next step is to understand how best to learn.

Many managers' inclination is to dive in and start talking to people. You will pick up much soft information this way, but this method is not efficient. Why? Because it can be time-consuming and because its lack of structure makes it difficult to know how much weight to place on various individuals' observations. Your views may be shaped excessively by the first few people (or last few) with whom you talk. And people may seek you out early precisely so they can influence you.

Thus, you should consider using a structured learning process designed for new leaders. To illustrate the advantages of a structured approach, imagine that you plan to meet with your direct reports to elicit their assessments of the situation. How might you go about doing this? Bringing them together right away might be a mistake, because some will hesitate to reveal their views in a public forum.

Instead, you decide to meet them one-on-one. Of course, this has its drawbacks too, because you have to meet people in some order. You should therefore expect that the people who are later on your schedule will be talking to the earlier ones to try to get a sense of what you are after. This may both reduce your ability to gain a range of views about what is going on and allow others to interpret your messages in ways you might not intend.

Suppose that you decide to meet with your direct reports one-on-one. In what order will you meet with them? And how will you avoid being excessively influenced by what the first couple of people say to you? One approach is to keep to the same "script" in all your meetings. Its format might consist of brief opening remarks about yourself and your approach, followed by questions about the other person (background, family, and interests) and then a standard set of questions about the business. This approach is powerful because the responses you get are comparable. You can line them up side by side and analyze what is consistent and inconsistent about the responses. This helps you gain insight into which people are being more or less open.

When diagnosing a new organization, start by meeting with your direct reports one-on-one. (This is an example of taking a horizontal slice across an organization by interviewing people at the same level in different functions.) Ask them essentially the same five questions:

1. What are the biggest challenges the organization is facing (or will face) in the near future?

2. Why is the organization facing (or going to face) these challenges?

3. What are the most promising unexploited opportunities for growth?

4. What would need to happen for the organization to exploit the potential of these opportunities?

5. If you were me, what would you focus attention on?

These five questions, coupled with careful listening and thoughtful follow-up, are certain to elicit many insights. By asking everyone the same set of questions, you can identify prevalent and divergent views, and thus avoid being swayed by the first or most forceful or articulate person you talk to. *How* people answer can also tell you a lot about your new team and its politics. Who answers directly and who is evasive or prone to going on tangents? Who takes responsibility and who points fingers? Who has a broad view of the business and who seems stuck in a silo?

Once you have distilled these early discussions into a set of observations, questions, and insights, convene your direct reports as a group, feed back your impressions and questions, and invite some discussion. You will learn more about both substance and team dynamics by doing so, and will simultaneously demonstrate how quickly you have begun to identify key issues.

You need not follow this process rigidly. You could, for example, get an outside consultant to do some diagnosis of the organization and feed back the results to your group (see "New Leader Assimilation Process"). Or you could invite an internal facilitator to run the process. The point is that even a modest amount of structure—a script and a sequence of interactions such as meeting with people individually, doing some analysis, and then meeting with them together—can dramatically accelerate your ability to extract actionable insights. Naturally, the questions you will ask will be tailored specifically for the groups you meet. If you are meeting with salespeople, for example,

## New Leader Assimilation Processes

One example of a structured learning method is the New Leader Assimilation Process originally developed by GE. In this process, each time a manager enters a significant new role, he or she is assigned a transition facilitator. The facilitator meets first with the new leader to lay out the process. This is followed by a meeting with the leader's new direct reports in which they are asked questions such as: What would you like to know about the new leader? What would you like him or her to know about you? about the business situation? The main findings are then fed back, without attribution, to the new leader. The process ends with a facilitated meeting between the new leader and the direct reports.

consider asking: What do our customers want that they are getting from our competitors and not getting from us?

Other structured learning methods are valuable in particular situations. Some of the methods described in table 2-1 may increase the efficiency of your learning process depending on your level in the organization and the type of business situation you are in. Effective new leaders employ a combination of methods, tailoring their learning strategy to the demands of the situation.

## Creating a Learning Plan

Your learning agenda defines *what* you want to learn. Your learning plan defines *how* you will go about learning it. It translates learning goals into specific sets of actions—identifying promising sources of insight and using systematic methods—that accelerate your learning. Your learning plan is a critical part of your overall

TABLE 2-1

## Structured Methods for Learning

| Method | Uses | Useful For |
|---|---|---|
| Organizational climate and employee satisfaction surveys | Learning about culture and morale. Many organizations do such surveys regularly, and a database may already be available. If not, consider setting up a regular survey of employee perceptions. | Useful for managers at all levels, if analysis is available specifically for your unit or group.<br>  Usefulness depends on how granular the collection and analysis is. This also assumes the survey instrument is a good one and the data have been collected carefully and analyzed rigorously. |
| Structured sets of interviews with "slices" of the organization or unit | Identifying shared and divergent perceptions of opportunities and problems. You can interview people at the same level in different departments (a horizontal slice) or bore down through multiple levels (a vertical slice). Whichever dimension you choose, ask everybody the same questions and look for similarities and differences in people's responses. | Most useful for managers leading groups of people from different functional backgrounds.<br>  Can be useful at lower levels if the unit is experiencing significant problems. |
| Focus groups | Probing issues that preoccupy key groups of employees, such as morale issues among frontline production or service workers. Gathering groups of people who work together also lets you see how they interact and who displays leadership. Fostering discussion promotes deeper insight. | Most useful for managers of large groups of people who perform a similar function, such as sales managers or plant managers.<br>  Can be useful for more senior managers as a way of getting some quick insights into the perceptions of key employee constituencies. |
| Analysis of critical past decisions | Illuminating decision-making patterns and sources of power and influence. Select an important recent decision and look into how it was made. Who exerted influence at each stage? Talk with people involved, probe their perceptions, and note what is and is not said. | Most useful for higher-level managers of business units or project groups. |

| Method | Uses | Useful For |
|---|---|---|
| Process analysis | Examining interactions among departments or functions and assessing the efficiency of a process. Select an important process, such as delivery of products to customers or distributors, and assign a cross-functional group to chart the process and identify bottlenecks and problems. | Most useful for managers of units or groups in which the work of multiple functional specialties must be integrated.  Can be useful for lower-level managers as a way of understanding how their groups fit into larger processes. |
| Plant and market tours | Plant tours are opportunities to meet production personnel informally and to listen to their concerns. Meetings with sales and production staff will help you assess technical capabilities. Market tours can introduce you to customers, whose comments can reveal problems and opportunities. | Most useful for managers of business units. |
| Pilot projects | Gaining deep insight into technical capabilities, culture, and politics. Though these insights are not the primary purpose of pilot projects, you can learn a lot from how the organization or group responds to your pilot initiatives. | Useful for managers at all levels. The size of the pilot projects and their impact will of course increase as one rises through the organization. |

90-day plan. In fact, as we will discuss later, learning should be a primary focus of your plan for your first 30 days on the job.

The heart of your learning plan is a cyclical learning process in which you collect information, analyze and distill it, develop hypotheses, and test them, thus progressively deepening your understanding of your new organization. Obviously, the specific insights you decide to pursue will vary from situation to situation. You can begin by looking critically at the learning plan template in the accompanying box and deciding which elements make sense for you, which do not, and what is missing. In the next chapter, we will explore different types of transition situations and return to the subject of what you need to learn and when.

---

**Learning Plan Template**

## Before Entry

- Read whatever you can find about the organization's strategy, structure, performance, and people.

- Look for external assessments of the performance of the organization. You will learn how knowledgeable, fairly unbiased people view the organization. If you are a manager at a lower level, talk to people who deal with your new group as suppliers or customers.

- Find external observers who know the organization well, including former employees, recent retirees, and people who have transacted business with the organization. Ask these people open-ended questions about the organization's history, politics, and culture. Talk with your predecessor if possible.

- Talk to your new boss.

- As you begin to learn about the organization, write down your first impressions and eventually some hypotheses.

- Compile an initial set of questions to guide your structured inquiry once you arrive.

## Soon After Entry

- Review detailed operating plans, performance data, and personnel data.

- Meet one-on-one with your direct reports and ask them the questions you compiled. You will learn about convergent and divergent views, and about them as people.

- Assess how things are going at key interfaces from the inside. You will hear how salespeople, purchasing agents, customer service representatives, and others perceive your organization's dealings with external constituencies. You will also learn about problems they see that others do not.

- Test strategic alignment from the top down. Ask people at the top what the company's vision and strategy are. Then see how far down into the organizational hierarchy those beliefs penetrate. You will learn how well the previous leader drove vision and strategy down through the organization.

- Test awareness of challenges and opportunities from the bottom up. Start by asking frontline people how they view the company's challenges and opportunities. Then work your way up. You will learn how well the people at the top check the pulse of the organization.

- Update your questions and hypotheses.

- Meet with your boss to discuss your hypotheses and findings.

### By the End of the First Month

- Gather your team to feed back your preliminary findings. You will elicit confirmations and challenges of your assessments, and will learn more about the group and its dynamics.

- Now analyze key interfaces from the outside in. You will learn how people on the outside (suppliers, customers, distributors, and others) perceive your organization and its strengths and weaknesses.

*(continued)*

**Learning Plan Template** *(continued)*

- Analyze a couple of key processes. Convene representatives of the responsible groups to map out and evaluate the processes you selected. You will learn about productivity, quality, and reliability.

- Meet with key integrators. You will learn how things work at interfaces among functional areas within the company. What problems do they perceive that others do not? Seek out the natural historians. They can fill you in on the history, culture, and politics of the organization, and they are also potential allies and influencers.

- Update your questions and hypotheses.

- Meet with your boss again to discuss your observations.

---

# Learning About Culture

Your most vexing business problems likely will have a cultural dimension. In some cases, you will find that aspects of the existing culture are key impediments to realizing high performance. You will thus have to struggle to change them. Other aspects of the culture will turn out to be functional and thus worthy of preservation. Having realized how proud and motivated the workforce was, Chris Bagley could draw on this energy to upgrade the plant. Think how much more difficult it would have been had he inherited a group of complacent, hostile people.

Because cultural habits and norms operate powerfully to reinforce the status quo, it is vital to diagnose problems in the existing culture and to figure out how to begin to address them. These assessments are particularly important if you are coming in from the outside or joining a unit within your existing organization that has a strong subculture.

You can't hope to change your organization's work culture if you don't understand it. One useful framework for analyzing an organization's work culture approaches it at three levels: symbols, norms, and assumptions.[1]

- *Symbols* are signs, including logos and styles of dress; they distinguish one culture from another and promote solidarity. Are there distinctive symbols that signify your unit and help members recognize one another?

- *Norms* are shared social rules that guide "right behavior." What behaviors get encouraged or rewarded in your unit? What elicits scorn or disapproval?

- *Assumptions* are the often-unarticulated beliefs that pervade and underpin social systems. These beliefs are the air that everyone breathes. What truths does everyone take for granted?

To understand a culture, you must peer below the surface of symbols and norms and get at underlying assumptions. To do this you need to carefully watch the way people interact with one another. For instance, do people seem most concerned with individual accomplishment and reward, or are they more focused on group accomplishment? Does the group seem more casual, or more formal? More aggressive and hard-driving, or more laid-back?

As my colleague Geri Augusto has noted, the most relevant assumptions for new leaders involve *power* and *value*.[2] Regarding power, key questions are as follows: Who do key people in your organization think can legitimately exercise authority and make decisions? What does it take to earn your stripes? Regarding value, what actions are believed by employees to create (and destroy) value? At White Goods, employees were proud of producing premium-quality products, so a decision to move downmarket could easily trigger resistance. Divergent assumptions about power and value—for example, between workers and managers—can complicate efforts to align the organization. Some degree of divergence is, of course, unavoidable. The danger comes when the gap becomes too wide to be bridged by effective communication and negotiation.

### Organizational, Professional, and Geographic Perspectives

You can also think about culture from three perspectives: organizational, professional, and geographic. As you read the following descriptions, imagine examining each aspect of culture through a camera's zoom lens. Start by zooming in to see organizational culture, then gradually widen your focus to see professional culture, and then focus broadly on geographic culture.

*Organizational Culture.* Cultures within organizations or groups develop over time, and can be deeply rooted. Organizational culture is expressed in the way people treat one another (friendly, formal, relaxed), the values they share (honesty, competitiveness, hard work), the routines they follow as they hold meetings and exchange information, and so on.

Organizational cultures vary within and across industries. For example, managers in an established, traditional consumer products company may be comfortable with more elaborate processes and systems than managers in a start-up in the same industry. An energy industry executive might feel he's on shaky ground working in a fashion retail company.

*Professional Culture.* Managers as a group also share cultural characteristics that distinguish them from other professional groups such as engineers, administrative assistants, and doctors or teachers. But this doesn't mean all managers are alike. In fact, you've probably seen huge cultural differences within and between business functions.

For example, financial managers have different worldviews than marketing or R&D managers. In part, this is because the people who gravitate toward these functions have different professional training.

*Geographic Culture.* Geographic changes can present the greatest diversity in culture. The way people do business in different regions of a country can vary significantly. Differences in business cultures between two countries are even more pronounced. For example, U.S. managers tend to work within a more individualistic culture, whereas Japanese managers stress more collectivist values and behaviors.

## Moving into New Cultures

If you're moving to a new company within the same industry, or to a new industry (from financial services to food management, for example), you'll likely confront organizational cultural changes.

Your new position may take you to a different functional arena (for example, from operations to marketing) or to a whole new level of responsibility (for instance, from a functional area to general management). In such cases, you will face professional cultural changes—differences that are significant even when you move to a new position within the same organization.

If you're taking a position with a division in your company that is located in a different city or region in your country, or in another country, you'll likely face geographic cultural changes.

These different kinds of culture change can overlap and reinforce one another (see figure 2-2). For instance, if you move to a new company that's also in a new city or region, you'll face organizational and geographic culture changes. It is useful to assess your culture adaptation challenge on a scale of

**FIGURE 2 - 2**

## Intersecting Dimensions of Culture

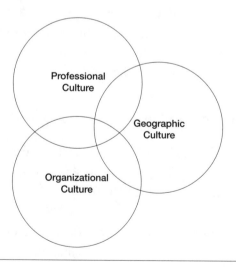

1 to 10 on each of these three dimensions. On the organizational culture dimension, a 10 would be a move from a highly centralized, process-focused organization to a highly decentralized, relationship-focused organization. On the professional culture dimension, a 10 would be a move from finance to human resources or vice versa. Finally, on the geographic dimension, a 10 would be a move from Minneapolis to Tokyo. If the total of these three numbers is 15 or greater, then you are facing a major cultural shift. To avoid missteps, you must devote significant energy to understanding and adapting to the new culture or cultures.

### Adaptation or Alteration?

After identifying the organizational culture to which you're moving, you need to decide whether to adapt to or alter that culture. Whatever your situation, you'll need to understand the impact of existing cultural characteristics on your new situation. In particular, you'll want to assess which cultural characteristics are helping performance, and which may be harming performance. Your future success depends on knowing the difference—and taking the proper action.

## Closing the Loop

Your learning priorities and strategies will inevitably shift as you dig deeper. As you start to interact with your new boss, or to figure out where to get some early wins, or to build supportive coalitions, it will be critical for you to gain additional insights. So plan to return to this chapter periodically to reassess your learning agenda and create new learning plans.

## ACCELERATION CHECKLIST

1. Are you effective at learning about new organizations? Do you sometimes fall prey to the action imperative? To coming in with "the answer"? If so, how will you avoid doing this?

2. What is your learning agenda? Based on what you know now, compose a list of questions to guide your early inquiry. If you have begun to form hypotheses about what is going on, what are they and how will you test them?

3. Given the questions you want to answer, which individuals are most likely to provide you with solid actionable insights?

4. How might you increase the efficiency of your learning process? What are some ways you might extract more actionable insights for your investment of time and energy?

5. Given your answers to the previous questions, start to create your learning plan.

# 3

# Match Strategy
# to Situation

WHEN CLAIRE WEEKS stepped into her new role as head of the industrial products division of a large multinational company, she believed the division had enough strength to continue to achieve double-digit earnings growth. Growth had been strong over the past four years, and the division had several promising products in the pipeline. Based on her early assessments, Claire committed herself to achieving the ambitious goals laid out in her predecessor's plan.

Claire soon discovered the situation was less rosy. The division's stellar past performance masked structural problems with pricing, inventories, and strained distributor relationships. It seemed that her predecessor had been mortgaging the division's future to make himself look good.

Although not mortal threats, these problems made it difficult for Claire to meet her targets. Rather than go to the CEO, explain the problems, and take the hit, however, she elected to push forward. She believed that she could eke out enough growth through price increases and acquisitions to keep results on track until a key new product was launched.

Struggling to achieve the goals she had committed herself to, Claire made a series of avoidable missteps that eroded her credibility. She alienated the company's distributors by forcing through price increases. She made a couple of bad calls trying to speed up critical new-product launches. As it became obvious that she would not meet her targets through organic growth, she tried and failed to make a significant acquisition. Claire's problems flowed from a mistaken diagnosis of the situation. Believing that she was in a sustaining-success situation, she signed on to overly ambitious growth targets. In reality, the company was in need of a significant realignment. Rather than confront the need for realignment and reset expectations, Claire became a victim of her own shortsightedness. She resigned when it became clear the CEO had lost confidence in her ability to lead the division.

Far too many new leaders like Claire Weeks do a poor job of diagnosing their situations and tailoring their strategies accordingly. Then, because they misunderstand the situation, they make unnecessary mistakes like Claire's commitment to unachievable earnings goals. This painful scenario continues to recur because people typically model their own transitions on a limited set of experiences.

If you're like Claire, you've learned to make transitions the hard way. You've made mistakes along the way, and you've learned from them. If you're fortunate, bosses, mentors, and advisers have shared their hard-won experience with you. Over time you've probably fixed on some "must do's" and "do not do's." It is worth being clear about them up front, so you can evaluate which hold up in your new situation and which do not. Consider taking some time to summarize your own rules of thumb for making a successful transition before you read further.

Now step back and assess how robust and actionable these insights are. Your recent move suggests that your approach has worked well up to this point, but it won't necessarily continue to work if you are moving to a different level or entering an unfamiliar business situation. Even if you have had broad exposure to managerial disciplines (marketing, operations, R&D, finance), your experience with different types of business situations (start-up, turnaround, realignment, and sustaining success) may still be narrow.

By methodically diagnosing the situation, Claire Weeks could have avoided her problems. *Matching your strategy to your situation* requires careful diagnosis of the business situation. Only then can you be clearheaded, not just about the challenges, but also about the opportunities and resources available to you.

## Diagnosing the Business Situation

The four broad types of business situations that new leaders must contend with are start-up, turnaround, realignment, and sustaining success. (From now on we will refer to this framework of transition types as the $ST_ARS$ model.) An outline of the characteristics of each of these types, and their associated challenges and opportunities, will help you to recognize the key structural features of your own situation.

What are the defining features of each of the four $ST_ARS$ situations? In a *start-up* you are charged with assembling the capabilities (people, funding, and technology) to get a new business, product, or project off the ground. In a *turnaround* you take on a unit or group that is recognized to be in trouble and work to get it back on track. Both start-ups and turn-arounds involve much resource-intensive construction work—there isn't much existing infrastructure and capacity for you to build on. To a significant degree, you get to start fresh. But both require that you start making tough calls early.

Realignments and sustaining-success situations, by contrast, are situations in which you enter organizations that have significant strengths, but also serious constraints on what you can and cannot do. In *realignment,* your challenge is to revitalize a unit, product, process, or project that is drifting into trouble. In a *sustaining-success* situation, you are shouldering responsibility for preserving the vitality of a successful organization and taking it to the next level. Put another way, in realignments you have to reinvent the business; in sustaining-success situations, you have to invent the challenge. In both situations, you typically have some time before you need to make major calls, which is good news because you have to learn a lot about the culture and politics and begin building supportive coalitions.

Applying these categories to business situations is useful regardless of your level in the organization. You may be a new CEO taking over an entire company that is in start-up mode. Or you could be a first-line supervisor managing a new production line, a brand manager launching a new product, an R&D team leader responsible for a new product-development project, or an information technology manager responsible for implementing a new enterprise software system. All of these situations share the characteristics of a start-up. Turnovers, realignments, and sustaining-success situations also arise at all levels, in companies large and small.

## Understanding the History

The relationships among these four business situations are depicted in the ST$_A$RS model of business evolution shown in figure 3-1. The key point is that businesses (and, for that matter, projects, processes, products, and plants) tend to move predictably from one type of situation to another. Understanding the history of your new organization will help you grasp the challenges and opportunities of your situation.

Let us start, fittingly, with start-ups. Successful start-ups grow and eventually become sustaining-success situations. Often the individuals who managed the start-up move on to tackle new start-ups, and managers more experienced at running larger

FIGURE 3 - 1

**The ST$_A$RS Model**

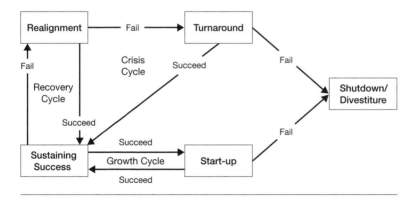

businesses take over. These successful businesses may in turn give birth to internal start-ups as they diversify into new products, services, processes, or technologies. In this way, healthy companies enter a *growth cycle.*

But entropy increases. Successful businesses tend, because of internal complacency or external challenges or both, to drift toward trouble. Even if the organization is not yet in crisis, acute observers see gathering storm clouds that signal a need for realignment. This was the situation facing Claire Weeks, who failed to recognize it early enough. Realigning an organization usually means redirecting its resources, such as by abandoning aging product lines and developing new technologies. It often means changing the organization's strategy, structure, skills, and even its culture in fundamental ways. Realigning the business returns it to a sustaining-success state, designated in the model as the *recovery cycle.* One of the main hurdles of realignment is that many in such organizations, like Claire Weeks, are in denial about the situation. They continue to believe they are sustaining success even as they are heading for trouble.

If efforts to realign the business fail, it can end as a full-scale turnaround. This happens when prior leaders failed to see the need for realignment. (After all, businesses rarely go directly from sustaining success to turnaround.) No matter why this happened, there is rarely argument about the need to make big changes fast if the situation is dire, the business is losing money, and its best talent is jumping ship. Turning around a failing business requires the new leader to cut it down to a defendable core fast and then begin to build it back up. This painful process, if successful, leaves the business in a sustaining-success situation, as illustrated by the *crisis cycle* in figure 3-1. If efforts to turn around the business fail, the result is shutdown or divestiture.

It is important to understand these cycles. You cannot figure out where to take a new organization if you do not understand where it has been and how it got where it is. In a realignment, for example, it is essential to understand what made the organization successful in the past and why it drifted into trouble. To understand your situation, you have to put on your historian's hat.

## Identifying Challenges and Opportunities

In all four of the ST$_A$RS situations, the eventual goal is the same: a successful and growing business. But each type of transition presents a distinct set of challenges. If you are succeeding the leader of a high-performing business, the challenge will be to take charge in your own way while preserving what is good about the organization. If you are in a start-up situation, such as getting a new product off the ground, *you* will be responsible for creating the organization. If you are in a realignment situation, you will have to build awareness of the need for change.

Each situation also presents characteristic opportunities that you can leverage to build momentum. In a turnaround situation, everyone realizes that changes need to be made quickly. That group awareness can help you move forward. In realignment situations such as Claire Weeks's, the organization is still likely to have strong people, products, and technologies. By finding these islands of excellence, you can marshal the building blocks to make needed changes.

Although every situation is unique, each of the four types of transitions exhibits distinct challenges and opportunities, summarized in table 3-1.

TABLE 3 - 1

## Challenges and Opportunities of Transition Types

| Transition Type | Challenges | Opportunities |
|---|---|---|
| Start-up | • Building structures and systems from scratch without a clear framework or boundaries.<br>• Welding together a cohesive high-performing team.<br>• Making do with limited resources. | • You can do things right from the beginning.<br>• People are energized by the possibilities.<br>• There is no preexisting rigidity in people's thinking. |
| Turnaround | • Reenergizing demoralized employees and other stakeholders.<br>• Handling time pressure and having a quick and decisive impact.<br>• Going deep enough with painful cuts and difficult personnel choices. | • Everyone recognizes that change is necessary.<br>• Affected constituencies (such as suppliers who want the company to stay in business) may offer significant external support.<br>• A little success goes a long way. |
| Realignment | • Dealing with deeply ingrained cultural norms that no longer contribute to high performance.<br>• Convincing employees that change is necessary.<br>• Restructuring the top team and refocusing the organization. | • The organization has significant pockets of strength.<br>• People want to continue to see themselves as successful. |
| Sustaining success | • Playing good defense by avoiding decisions that cause problems.<br>• Living in the shadow of a revered leader and dealing with the team he or she created.<br>• Finding ways to take the business to the next level. | • A strong team may already be in place.<br>• People are motivated to succeed.<br>• Foundations for continued success (such as the product pipeline) may be in place. |

## Transforming Organizational Psychology

People's attitudes and emotions vary in predictable ways depending on which of the ST$_A$RS situations they are experiencing. Participants in a start-up are likely to be more excited and hopeful than members of a troubled group facing failure. But at the same time, employees of a start-up are typically much less focused on key issues than those in a turnaround, simply because the vision, strategy, structures, and systems that channel organizational energy are not yet in place. Participants in a turnaround often know what the problems are, but not what to do about them.

Success at transitioning therefore depends, in part, on your ability to transform the prevailing organizational psychology in predictable ways. In start-ups, the prevailing mood is often one of excited confusion, and your job is to channel that energy into productive directions, in part by deciding what not to do. In turnarounds, you may be dealing with a group of people who are close to despair; it is your job to provide a light at the end of the tunnel. In realignments, you will likely have to pierce through the veil of denial that is preventing people from confronting the need to reinvent the business. Finally, in sustaining-success situations, you have to "invent the challenge" by finding ways to keep people motivated, to combat complacency, and to find new direction for growth—both organizational and personal.

## Leading with the Right Skills

The management skills necessary for success vary among the four ST$_A$RS situations. Start-ups and turnarounds call for "hunters," people who can move fast and take chances. In turn-arounds, for example, the premium is on rapid diagnosis of the business situation (markets, technologies, products, strategies) and then aggressive moves to cut back the organization to a defendable core. You will need to act quickly and decisively, often on the basis of incomplete information.

The skills that contribute to success in realignment and sustaining-success situations, by contrast, are more akin to farming than hunting. More subtle influence skills come into play: Skilled farmers focus on understanding the culture and politics of the organization. They also painstakingly cultivate awareness of the need for change, by promoting shared diagnosis, influencing opinion leaders, and encouraging benchmarking.

To put it another way, in turnarounds the problems teach the people about the need for major changes. In realignments, by contrast, *you* must teach people about the problems. Turn-arounds are also ready-fire-aim situations: You make the tough calls with less than full knowledge and then adjust as you learn more. Realignments (and sustaining-success assignments) are ready-aim-fire situations. Time urgency is less extreme, but it is more important to understand the organization, get the strategy right and build support for it, and make some good early calls.

Because of their differing imperatives, it is easy for hunters to stumble in realignment and sustaining-success situations and for farmers to stumble in start-ups and turnarounds. The experienced turnaround person facing a realignment is at risk of arriving with "the answer" and moving too fast, needlessly causing resistance. The experienced realignment person in a turn-around situation is at risk of moving too slowly, expending energy on cultivating consensus when it is unnecessary to do so, thus squandering precious time.

This is not to say that people who are good at hunting cannot farm or vice versa. Good managers can succeed in all four of the $ST_ARS$ situations, though no one is equally good at all of them. But it is essential to think hardheadedly about which of your skills and inclinations will serve you well in your particular situation and which are likely to get you into trouble. Don't arrive with your spear if you need to be plowing.

## Focusing Your Energy

Achieving clarity about the type of situation you are confronting helps you decide what you need to do in your first 90 days. In particular, clarity helps you to make three fundamental early choices:

1. How much emphasis will you place on learning as opposed to doing?

2. How much emphasis will you place on offense as opposed to defense?

3. What should you do to get some early wins?

### Learning Versus Doing

How much time should you devote to deepening your understanding of your new organization as opposed to making decisions, initiating changes, recruiting new people, and so on? The correct balance of learning and doing differs strikingly in the four $ST_ARS$ situations. In turnarounds and start-ups, the premium is on doing. You have to make some early calls without full information. If you spend too much time learning, events will overtake you and create a vicious cycle. You will have to fire before you are certain of your aim and then adjust accordingly.

This is not to say that learning is unimportant in turn-arounds and start-ups. But the learning required in these situations is fundamentally technical in nature. It is about mastering quickly what there is to know about the technical domain of the organization—products, markets, projects, technologies, and strategies. This is the easiest and fastest type of learning.

In realignments and sustaining-success situations, a different emphasis on learning is warranted early on, because you are dealing with people who are, or think they are, successful. They may not be hungry for change or for direction from you. Early mistakes, especially if they are interpreted as risking the traditional strengths of the business, will cost you dearly. The good news is that you will have time to learn. There is no need for urgent early action in realignments or sustaining-success situations. You can afford to aim carefully before you fire your first critical shots.

In realignments and sustaining-success situations, you must delve deeply into organizational culture and politics. If, as was the case with Chris Bagley in the last chapter, you spend inadequate time understanding these dimensions of the organization, you will inevitably step on some land mines. As you have seen, learning about organizational politics and culture is hard work and takes time. Fortunately, you will have time if you give yourself permission to move cautiously and don't fall prey, as Claire Weeks did, to the action imperative.

### Offense Versus Defense

Early on, how much time should you spend on offensive planning—identifying new markets and developing new products and technologies—and how much on playing good defense—defending existing market share positions, buttressing existing positions, and extending existing products?

Of course, you need to do both in all of these situations. But the relative emphasis you should initially place on offense and defense differs greatly. For example, a start-up is all about offense: You are there to get something new going, and there is usually nothing to defend. In a turnaround, by contrast, the early imperative is good defense. You need to identify the remaining strengths of the organization and cut back to this defendable core that can help generate financial resources to support your next moves. Only then can you shift to offense and begin identifying and developing new platforms for growth.

Realignments and sustaining-success situations differ comparably. In a realignment, the agenda is to make midcourse corrections that take the business in new directions. You will still want to defend existing markets, but your best energies should be spent on the new offensive plan. In sustaining-success situations, the key is to play good defense early on, so you don't risk the crown jewels. Over time, you can gradually shift your attention to how you will take the organization to a new level.

Figure 3-2 depicts a matrix that summarizes where the early focus of energy should be in the four business situations.

**FIGURE 3 - 2**

**Focusing Your Energy**

|  | More Offense | More Defense |
|---|---|---|
| **More Learning** | Realignment | Sustaining Success |
| **More Doing** | Start-up | Turnaround |

### Securing Early Wins

To build momentum in your new job, you have to get some early wins. But what a "win" is differs dramatically among the four situations. In a start-up, getting the right team in place and achieving strategic focus are key wins. Critically, you have to decide what you are *not* going to do—and then you have to discipline your organization not to do it. In turnarounds, getting the right team in place is also a key potential early win, as is identifying the defendable core of the business and making major progress in paring the organization back to it. In realignments, gaining acceptance of the need for change and instilling a sense of urgency are often big early wins. Finally, in sustaining-success situations, gaining and displaying understanding of what has made the organization successful is a key early win, because it helps you win the right to make decisions about the organization's future.

## Diagnosing Your Portfolio

Your situation is unlikely to be a pure and tidy example of a start-up, turnaround, realignment, or sustaining-success situation. At a high level your situation may fit reasonably neatly into one of these categories. But as soon as you drill down, you will almost certainly discover that you are managing a portfolio—of products, projects, processes, plants, or people—that represents a mix of $ST_ARS$ situations. For instance, you may be taking over an organization that enjoys incremental growth with successful products and in which one group is launching a line of products based on a new technology. Or you may be working to turn around a company that has a couple of high-performing state-of-the-art plants.

Your final diagnostic step, then, is to figure out which parts of your new organization belong in each of the four ST$_A$RS categories. This exercise will help you to think systematically about challenges and opportunities in each piece. It will also supply you a common language with which to talk to your new team about why and how you are going to manage various pieces differently.

Take some time to assign the pieces in your new portfolio (products, processes, projects, plants, and people) to the four categories using the figure 3-3. Given this arrangement, how will you manage the various pieces differently? What do you need from them? What do they need from you?

FIGURE 3 - 3

**Diagnosing Your Portfolio**

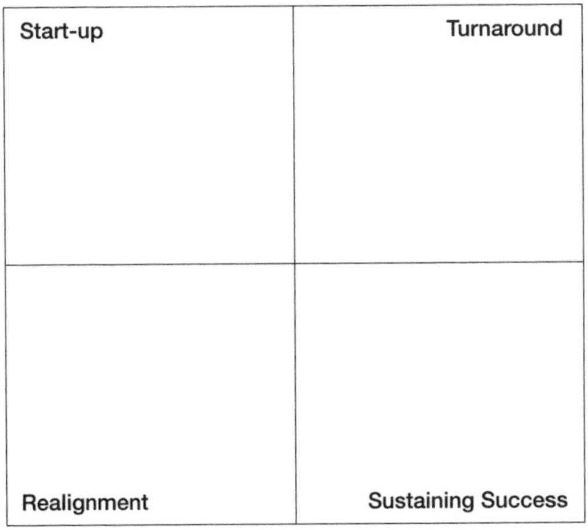

| Start-up | Turnaround |
|---|---|
|  |  |
| Realignment | Sustaining Success |

## Rewarding Success

The ST$_A$RS framework has implications for how you should evaluate and reward the people who work for you. When groups of new leaders are asked to predict which type of transition is rewarded best and which the least when performed successfully in their organizations, turnarounds typically emerge as the best rewarded and realignments the least.

This is not surprising. A successful turnaround is a visible and easily measurable individual accomplishment, as is a successful start-up. In a realignment, by contrast, success consists of avoiding disaster. It is hard to measure results in a realignment—it is the dog that does not bite. Also, success requires painstakingly building awareness of the need for change—which often means giving credit to the group rather than taking it yourself. As for rewarding sustaining success, people seldom call their local power company to say, "Thanks for keeping the lights on today." But if the power goes off, the screaming is immediate and loud.

There is a paradox inherent in rewarding people most lavishly for successfully turning around failing businesses. Few high-potential leaders show much interest in realignments, preferring the action and recognition associated with turnarounds (and start-ups). So who exactly is responsible for preventing businesses from becoming turnarounds? And does the fact that companies reward turnarounds (and do not know how to reward realignments) make it more likely that businesses will end in crisis in the first place? Skilled managers can seemingly count on less-accomplished people to mess up businesses so they can come charging to the rescue. Claire Weeks's successor looked like a genius.

The more general point, of course, is that performance must be rewarded differently in the different ST$_A$RS situations. The performance of people put in charge of start-ups and turn-arounds is easiest to evaluate, because you can focus on measurable outcomes relative to some clear prior baseline.

Evaluating success and failure in realignment and sustaining-success situations is much more problematic. Performance in a realignment may be better than expected, but still poor. Or it may be that nothing much seems to happen, because a crisis was avoided. Sustaining-success situations pose similar problems. Success may consist of a small loss of market share in the face of concerted attack by competitors or the eking out of a few percentage points of top-line growth in a mature business. The unknown in both realignments and sustaining-success situations is what would have happened if other actions had been taken or other people had been in charge—the "as compared to what" problem. Measuring success in such situations is much more work, because you have to have a deep understanding of the challenges new leaders face and the actions they are taking in order to assess the adequacy of their responses.

## Adopting 4-D Development

Finally, consider using the ST$_A$RS framework as a basis for selecting and developing people in your organization. This should be part of a broader, four-dimensional approach to high-potential talent development. The four dimensions are:

1. Managerial functions

2. Geographic regions

3. Career crossroads

4. ST$_A$RS business situations

Leading companies work hard to broaden the experience of their high-potential people along dimensions 1 and 2: exposure to diverse *management functions* (for example, marketing, operations, human resources, and finance) and to *international experience* (through overseas placements). Increasingly, companies are also managing leadership development along a third dimension—preparing managers for critical *crossroads* in their professional lives. As Ram Charan and his colleagues have noted, managers face critical breakpoints as they move from being first-time managers to managers of managers and all the way up to enterprise managers.[1] As they move from one level to another, the rules and skill requirements change in significant ways.

The fourth dimension of high-potential leadership development, breadth of exposure to different *ST$_A$RS business situations,* should be directly addressed in succession and development planning. Do you want to develop different horses for different courses—for example, specialists in turnarounds and start-ups? Or do you want to develop people who can hunt and farm in a wide range of business situations? If the former, you should select specialists with the right inclinations and give them increasing responsibilities in those specific situations. If the latter, then your future general managers should get experience with a spectrum of business situations, and you should coach them in how to succeed in each.

A related issue is how best to bring in new people from outside the organization. Suppose you are planning to hire a high-potential person away from a competitor. Which of the four ST$_A$RS situations would be most likely to set up that person to fail? The answer is realignment, because the new leader is put in the position of trying to convince people with whom he once competed that they are not as good as they think they are. It would be surprising if the new leader were not resented, and insiders who thought they should have gotten the job will be sharpening their knives. Without the right attention and support, the likelihood that this person will fail is high.

### ACCELERATION CHECKLIST

1. Which of the four $ST_ARS$ situations are you facing— start-up, turnaround, realignment, or sustaining success?

2. What are the implications for the challenges and opportunities you are likely to confront and for how you should approach accelerating your transition?

3. What are the implications for your learning agenda? Do you only need to understand the technical side of the business, or is it critical that you understand culture and politics as well?

4. Which of your skills and strengths are likely to be most valuable in your new situation and which have the potential to get you into trouble?

5. What is the prevailing frame of mind? What psychological transformations do you need to make and how will you bring them about?

6. Should your early focus be on offense or defense?

7. When you dig deeper, what is the mix of types of situations that you are managing? Which portions of your unit are in start-up, turnaround, realignment, and sustaining-success modes? What are the implications for how you should manage and reward the people who work for you?

4

# Secure Early Wins

WHEN ELENA LEE was promoted to head
the telephone customer-service unit of a
leading retailer, she was determined to
change the punitive, authoritarian managerial style of her predecessor. In her former job, she had been responsible for a
smaller group in the same organization, so she knew a lot about
the problems her new unit had been facing with quality of service. Convinced that she could dramatically improve performance through more employee participation and innovation,
she saw cultural change as her top priority.

Elena began by communicating her goals to employees. In a
series of memos and small-group meetings, she laid out her
vision for a more participative, more problem-solving culture.
These overtures met with skepticism from frontline employees
and outright dismissal by some supervisors.

Her next step was to begin twice-weekly meetings with supervisors to review unit performance and seek input on how to
improve it. Elena stressed that "the punishment culture is a
thing of the past" and that she expected supervisors to coach

employees. Cases involving discipline, she said, should be referred (on an interim basis) directly to her.

Over time Elena learned which supervisors were adjusting to the new arrangements and which were continuing to be punitive. She then conducted formal performance reviews and put two of the most recalcitrant supervisors on performance-improvement plans. One left almost immediately. The other shaped up acceptably.

Meanwhile, Elena focused on a critical aspect of the business: evaluation of customer satisfaction and the quality of service. She appointed her best supervisor and a couple of promising frontline people to a process-improvement team and asked them to produce a plan to introduce new performance metrics and a nonpunitive monitoring and coaching process. After tutoring them on how to pursue this project, she regularly reviewed their progress. When they presented recommendations, she promptly implemented them on a pilot basis in the section previously overseen by the departed supervisor. Elena promoted the most promising person on the process-improvement team to supervise that section and to take ownership of the pilot program.

By the end of her first year, Elena had extended the new process throughout the unit. Quality had improved substantially, and climate surveys revealed striking improvements in morale and employee satisfaction. Elena Lee succeeded in quickly creating momentum and building personal credibility. *Early wins* are the key to proving yourself quickly, as Dan Ciampa and I stressed in *Right from the Start*.[1] By the end of your transition, you want your boss, your peers, and your subordinates to feel that something new, something good, is happening. Early wins excite and energize people and build your personal credibility. Done well, early wins help you to create value for your new organization earlier and therefore reach the breakeven point much more quickly.

## Avoiding Common Traps

It is crucial to get early wins, but it is also important to secure them in the right way. Above all, of course, you want to avoid early losses, because it is tough to recover once the tide is running against you. These are the most common traps that afflict unwary new leaders:

- **Failing to focus.** It is all too easy to take on too much during a transition, and the results can be ruinous. You can end like Steven Leacock's befuddled horseman, who "flung himself on his horse and rode off madly in all directions."[2] You cannot hope to achieve results in more than a couple of areas during your transition. Thus, it is essential to identify promising opportunities and then focus relentlessly on translating them into wins.

- **Not taking the business situation into account.** What constitutes an early win will differ dramatically from one business situation to another. Simply getting people to talk about the organization and its challenges can be a big accomplishment in a realignment but a waste of time in a turnaround. Think tactically about what will build momentum best. Will it be a demonstrated willingness to listen and learn? Will it be rapid, decisive calls on pressing business issues?

- **Not adjusting for the culture.** Leaders who come into an organization from the outside are most at risk of stumbling into this trap. Having absorbed a different organization's culture, they bring with them its view of what a win is and how it is achieved. In some companies, a win has to be a visible individual accomplishment. In others, individual pursuit of glory, even if it achieves good results, is viewed as grandstanding and destructive of teamwork. In team-oriented organizations, early wins could come in the form of leading a team in the development of a new product idea or being viewed as a solid contributor and team player in a broader initiative. Be sure you understand what your organization does and does not view as a win.

- **Failing to get wins that matter to your boss.** It is essential to get early wins that energize your direct reports and other employees. But your boss's opinion about your accomplishments is critically important too. Even if you do not fully endorse his or her priorities, you have to make them central in thinking through what early wins you will aim for. Addressing problems that your boss cares about will go a long way toward building credibility and cementing your access to resources.

- **Letting your means undermine your ends.** Process matters. If you achieve impressive results in a manner that is seen as manipulative, underhanded, or inconsistent with the culture, you are setting yourself up for trouble. An early win that is accomplished in a way that exemplifies the behavior you hope to instill in your new organization is a double win.

# Making Waves (of Change)

Let us look at how the first few months of your transition fit into the larger picture of your full tenure in the new position. In a study of new general managers in various company settings, Jack Gabarro found that they typically plan and implement change in distinct "waves," illustrated in figure 4-1.[3] Following an early period of acclimatization, they began an early wave of changes. The pace then slowed to allow consolidation and deeper learning about the organization, and to allow people to catch their breath. Armed with more insight, the new general managers then implemented deeper, more thoroughgoing and structural wave of change. A final, less extreme wave focused on fine-tuning to maximize performance. By this point, most of these leaders were ready to move on.

**FIGURE 4 - 1**

## Waves of Change

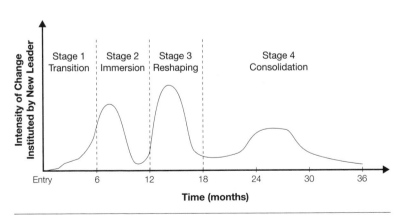

Gabarro's work has intriguing implications for managing transitions. First and most obviously, it suggests that you should devise your plan to secure early wins with your ends clearly in mind. The transition period lasts only a few months, but you will typically remain in the same job for two to four years before moving on to a new position. This two- to four-year period is your era in the organization, during which you will transition, make changes, and pursue your goals. To the greatest extent possible, your early wins should advance these longer-term goals.

### Planning Your Waves

In planning for your transition and beyond, it can be clarifying to plan to make successive waves of change. Each wave ought to consist of distinct phases: learning, designing the changes, building support, implementing the changes, and observing results. Thinking this way can release you to spend time up front to learn and prepare, and afterward to consolidate and get ready for the next wave. If you keep changing things, it is impossible to figure out what is working and what is not. Unending change is also a surefire recipe for burning out your people.

The goal of the first wave of change is to secure early wins. The new leader tailors early initiatives to build personal credibility, establish key relationships, and identify and harvest low-hanging fruit—the highest-potential opportunities for short-term improvements in organizational performance. Done well, this helps the new leader to build momentum and deepen his or her own learning.

The second wave of change addresses more fundamental issues of strategy, structure, systems, and skills to reshape the organization. This is when the real gains in organizational performance are achieved. But you will not get there if you do not secure early wins in the first wave.

### Matching Strategy to Situation

Patterns of change differ radically with the different $ST_ARS$ situations. How would you expect the pace and intensity of waves of change to differ in start-up, turnaround, realignment, and sustaining-success situations? In more time-critical situations—start-ups and turnarounds—you should expect to begin your first wave of change earlier. The intensity of change, as perceived by people in the organization, will also probably be greater. In realignment and sustaining-success situations, you can afford to take more time to learn and plan. If the business is genuinely in a sustaining-success situation, you might plan several modest waves of change rather than a single big bang.

## Establishing Long-Term Goals

In the first 90 days, a key goal is to build personal credibility and create organizational momentum. You do this by securing some early wins. Early wins leverage your energy and expand the potential scope of your subsequent actions.

As you look for ways to create momentum, keep in mind that the actions you take to get early wins should do double duty. Plan your early wins so they help you build credibility in the short run *and* lay a foundation for your longer-term goals. Specifically, your efforts to secure early wins should (1) be consistent with your A-item business priorities, and (2) introduce the new patterns of behavior you want to instill in the organization. In other words, the process of pinpointing the early wins you want to go after begins with thinking about the longer-term changes you want to realize by the end of your era.

## Focusing on Business Priorities and Behavioral Changes

Your long-term goals should consist of A-item business priorities and desired changes in the behavior of people in your organization. A-item priorities constitute the destination you are striving to reach in terms of measurable business objectives. This destination could be double-digit profit growth or a dramatic cut in defects and rework. For Elena Lee, one A-item priority was significant improvements in customer satisfaction. The point is to define your goals so you can lead with a distinct endpoint in mind.

Think about your legacy here. What do you want it to be? What do you want the letter announcing your promotion to your next job to say about what you did in this one? (It is a useful exercise to write this letter. What would you want people to say about your achievements in this job at the end of two to three years?)

## Defining Your A-Item Priorities

How do you select your A-item priorities? You may have no choice—your boss may simply hand them to you. But if you are able to shape your own agenda, or if think you need to negotiate goals with your boss, these guidelines may prove useful:

- **A-item priorities should follow naturally from core problems.** Establishing A-item priorities calls for pinpointing the critical areas in your organization that demand attention, as well as those that offer the greatest opportunities to contribute to dramatic improvement in performance. Elena Lee did this when she identified service quality as both a critical driver of performance and a goal that she could rally employees around. She might establish an A-item priority to increase customer satisfaction by 60 percent in one year.

- **A-item priorities should be neither too general nor too specific.** They should address several levels of specificity so you can establish measures and milestones along the way. For example, if your A-item priority is to condense the time it takes to get a new product from concept to customer, you should develop more specific, measurable short-term steps to mark your progress toward that goal. At the same time, it probably isn't helpful to define daily goals for improving time to market.

- **A-item priorities should offer clear direction yet allow for flexibility while you learn more about your situation.** The process of defining your A-item priorities is iterative. You need to have a clear set of goals early on, but you must often test, refine, and restate those goals. You have to remain open to adjusting your objectives as you move along. For example, if you decide the distribution system is a key target for improvement, you might make it an A-item priority to get products to customers 50 percent faster than before by the end of eighteen months. This goal is ambitious, so success would have a big impact. But it also is broad enough that you have some flexibility to figure out how and where you will achieve it, as you learn more.

**Targeting Behavioral Changes**

If A-item goals are the destination, then the behavior of people in your organization is a key part of how you do (or don't) get there. Put another way, if you are to achieve your A-item priorities by the end of your era, you may have to address dysfunctional patterns of behavior.

Start by identifying the unwanted behaviors. For example, Elena Lee wanted to reduce the fear and disempowerment in her organization. Then work out, as Elena did, a clear vision of how you would like people to behave by the end of your tenure in the job, and plan how your actions in pursuit of early wins will advance the process of behavior change. What behaviors do people in your organization consistently display that undermine the potential for high performance? Take a look at table 4-1, which lists some common but problematic behavior patterns, and then summarize your thoughts about the behaviors you would like to change.

# Securing Early Wins

Armed with an understanding of your A-item priorities and objectives for behavior change, you can proceed to create detailed plans for how you will secure early wins during your first 90 days and beyond. You should think about what you need to do in two phases: building credibility in the first 30 days and deciding where you will focus your energy to achieve early performance improvements in the following 60 days.

TABLE 4 - 1

## Problematic Behavior Patterns

| Lack of . . . | Symptoms |
|---|---|
| Focus | • The group can't clearly define its priorities, or it has too many priorities.<br>• Resources are spread too thin, leading to frequent crises and firefighting. People are rewarded for their ability to put out fires, not for devising enduring solutions. |
| Discipline | • People exhibit great variation in their levels of performance.<br>• Employees don't understand the negative consequences of inconsistency.<br>• People make excuses when they fail to meet commitments. |
| Innovation | • The group uses internal benchmarks to measure performance.<br>• Improvements in products and processes unfold slowly and incrementally.<br>• Employees are rewarded for maintaining stable performance, not for pushing the envelope. |
| Teamwork | • Team members compete with one another and protect turf rather than working together to achieve collective goals.<br>• People are rewarded for creating fiefdoms. |
| Sense of urgency | • Team members ignore the needs of external and internal customers.<br>• Complacency reigns, revealed in beliefs such as "We're the best and always have been" and "It doesn't matter if we respond immediately; it won't make any difference." |

## Building Credibility

In your first few weeks in your new job, you cannot hope to have a measurable impact on performance, but you can score small victories and signal that things are changing. Your objective at this early stage is to build personal credibility.

Because your earliest actions will have a disproportionate influence on how you are perceived, think through how you will get "connected" to your new organization. What messages do you want to get across about who you are and what you represent? What are the best ways to convey those messages? Identify your key audiences—direct reports, other employees, key outside constituencies—and craft a few messages tailored to each. These need not be about what you plan to do; that's premature. They should focus instead on who you are, the values and goals you represent, your style, and how you plan to conduct business.

Think about modes of engagement too. *How* will you introduce yourself? Should your first meetings with direct reports be one-on-one or in a group? Will these meetings be informal get-to-know-you sessions or will they immediately focus on business issues and assessment? What other channels, such as e-mail and video, will you use to introduce yourself more widely? Will you have early meetings at other locations where your organization has facilities?

As you make progress in getting connected, identify and act as quickly as you can to remove minor but persistent irritants in your new organization. Focus on strained external relationships and begin to repair them. Cut out redundant meetings, shorten excessively long ones, or improve physical-space problems. All this helps you to build personal credibility early on.

When you arrive, people will rapidly begin to assess you and your capabilities. Your credibility, or lack of it, will depend on how people in the organization would answer the following questions about you:

- Do you have the insight and steadiness to make tough decisions?

- Do you have values that they relate to, admire, and want to emulate?

- Do you have the right kind of energy?

- Do you demand high levels of performance from yourself and others?

For better or worse, they will begin to form opinions based on little data. Your early actions, good and bad, will shape perceptions. Once opinion about you has begun to harden, it is difficult to change. And the opinion-forming process happens remarkably quickly.

So how do you build personal credibility? In part it is about marketing yourself effectively, much akin to building equity in a brand. You want people to associate you with attractive capabilities, attitudes, and values. There's no single right answer for how to do this. In general, though, new leaders are perceived as more credible when they are

- **demanding but able to be satisfied.** Effective leaders press people to make realistic commitments and then hold them to those promises. But if you are never satisfied, you'll sap people's motivation.

- **accessible but not too familiar.** Being accessible does not mean making yourself available indiscriminately. It means being approachable, but in a way that preserves your authority.

- **decisive but judicious.** New leaders communicate their capacity to take charge without jumping too quickly into decisions that they are not ready to handle. Early in your transition, you want to project decisiveness but defer important decisions until you know enough to make them.

- **focused but flexible.** Avoid setting up a vicious cycle and alienating others by coming across as rigid and unwilling to consider multiple solutions to a problem. Effective new leaders establish authority by zeroing in on issues but consulting others and encouraging input.

- **active without causing commotion.** There's a fine line between building momentum and overwhelming your group or unit. Make things happen, but avoid pushing people to the point of burnout.

- **willing to make tough calls but humane.** You may have to make tough calls right away, including letting marginal performers go. Effective new leaders do what needs to be done, but they do it in ways that preserve peoples' dignity and that others perceive as fair.

### Leveraging "Teachable Moments"

Your actions during your first few weeks in the organization will have symbolic resonance. To illustrate this, consider the experience of Lara Moore, who took over an underperforming unit at a major financial services company. Based on her early diagnosis, Lara knew the unit suffered from a severe case of bureaucratic sclerosis. This problem was symbolized by the floor-to-ceiling filing cabinets that her predecessor had maintained, documenting all his transactions and decisions, however trivial. One of Lara's first acts was to have all these cabinets removed, as people in the office looked on in amazement.

Early actions often get transformed into stories, which can define you as hero or villain. Do you take the time to informally introduce yourself to the support staff or do you focus only on your boss, peers, and direct reports? Something as simple as this can help to brand you as "accessible" or "remote." How you introduce yourself to the organization, how you treat support staff, how you deal with small irritants—all of these pieces of behavior can become the kernels of stories that circulate widely. To nudge the mythology in a positive direction, look for and leverage *teachable moments*. These are actions—such as the way that Elena Lee dealt with recalcitrant supervisors—that clearly display what you are about; they also model the kinds of behavior you want to encourage. They need not be dramatic statements or confrontations. It can be as simple, and as hard, as asking the penetrating question that crystallizes your group's understanding of some key problem they are confronting.

### Securing Tangible Results

Building personal credibility and developing some key relationships helps you get some immediate wins. Soon, however, you should be identifying opportunities to get some quick, tangible performance improvement in the business. The best candidates are problems that you can tackle reasonably quickly with modest expenditure and that will yield visible operational and financial gains. Examples include bottlenecks that restrict productivity and incentive programs that undermine performance by causing conflict.

Identify two or three key areas, at most, where you will seek to achieve rapid improvement. If you take on too many initiatives, you risk losing focus. But don't put all your eggs in one basket. Think about risk management: Build a promising portfolio of early-win initiatives so that big successes in one will balance disappointments in others. Then focus relentlessly on getting results.

To set the stage for securing early wins, your learning agenda should specifically address how you will identify promising opportunities for improvement. To translate your goals into specific initiatives to secure early wins, work through the following guidelines:

- **Keep your long-term goals in mind.** The actions that you take to secure early wins should, to the greatest extent possible, serve your A-item priorities and long-term goals for behavior change.

- **Identify a few promising focal points.** Focal points are areas or processes (such as the customer service processes for Elena Lee) where improvement can dramatically strengthen the organization's overall operational or financial performance. Other examples of focal points might include a mutual fund company's process for reporting to the Securities and Exchange Commission or a pharmaceutical company's handoff from research to marketing.

- **Concentrate on the most promising focal points.** Mastering a few focal points you identify will reduce the time and energy needed to achieve tangible results. Improving performance early in these areas will win you freedom and space to pursue more extensive changes.

- **Launch pilot projects.** Design promising pilot initiatives, targeted at your chosen focal points, that you can undertake right away. Successful early projects set your overall plan in motion, energize your people, and yield real improvements. This is what Elena Lee did first to begin to improve customer service in her new organization.

- **Elevate change agents.** Identify the people in your new unit, at all levels, who have the insight, drive, and incentives to advance your agenda. Promote them, as

Elena Lee did, to positions of increasing responsibility. Then send a message to everyone else by rewarding them lavishly for success.

- **Leverage the pilot projects to introduce new behaviors.** Your early pilot projects, like Elena Lee's, should serve as models of how you want your organization, unit, or group to function in the future. Use the checklist in the accompanying box to help plan pilot projects with maximum impact.

---

### Pilot Project Checklist

For each pilot project you set up to secure early wins, use this checklist to be sure you are setting high standards for the kinds of behavior you want to encourage.

- What is the right mix of people, in terms of knowledge, skills, and personal chemistry?
- Who has the credibility, the project management skills, and the creativity to lead the project?
- What are achievable "stretch" goals?
- What are achievable deadlines?
- What coaching or framework will you provide to guide team problem solving and decision making?
- What other resources are necessary for success?
- How will you hold people accountable for achieving superior results?
- How will you reward success?

---

### Avoiding Predictable Surprises

All your efforts to secure early wins could come to naught if you don't pay attention to identifying ticking time bombs and preventing them from exploding in your face. If they do explode, your focus will instantly shift to continuous firefighting, and your hopes for systematically getting established and building momentum will fly out the window.

Some bolts from the blue really do come out of the blue. When this happens, you simply have to gird your loins and mount the best crisis response that you can. But far more often new leaders are taken off track by what my colleague Max Bazerman and I call "predictable surprises." These are situations in which people have all the information necessary to identify the problem and take corrective action but fail to do so.[4]

This often happens because the new leader simply doesn't look in the right places or ask the right questions. As discussed in chapter 1, we have preferences about the types of problems we like to work on and those we prefer to avoid or don't feel competent to address. If you are a marketing person and are taking on leadership of a new product launch team, it would not be surprising if you focused more on the marketing aspects than on the manufacturing ramp-up. But you will also have to discipline yourself either to dig into areas in which you are not fully comfortable or to find trustworthy people with the necessary expertise to do so.

Another reason for predictable surprises is that different parts of the organization have different pieces of the puzzle, but no one puts them together. Every organization has its information silos. If you don't put processes in place to make sure that critical information is surfaced and integrated, then you are putting yourself at risk of being predictably surprised.

Use the following set of questions to identify areas where potential problems may be lurking:

- **External environment.** Could trends in public opinion, government action, or economic conditions precipitate major problems for your unit? Examples: A change in government policy that favors competitors or unfavorably influences your prices or costs; a major shift in public opinion about the health or safety implications of using your product; an emerging economic crisis in a developing country.

- **Customers, markets, competitors, and strategy.** Are there developments in the competitive situation confronting your organization that could pose major challenges? Examples: A study suggesting that your product is inferior to that of a competitor; a new competitor that is offering a lower-cost substitute; a price war.

- **Internal capabilities.** Are there potential problems with your unit's processes, skills, and capabilities that could precipitate a crisis? Examples: An unexpected loss of key personnel; major quality problems at a key plant; a product recall.

- **Organizational politics.** Are you in danger of unwittingly stepping on a political land mine? Examples: Certain people in your unit are "untouchable," but you don't know it; you fail to recognize that a key peer is subtly undermining you.

## Leading Change

As you work out where to get your early wins, think about how you are going to make change happen in your organization.

### Planned Change Versus Collective Learning

Once you have identified the most important problems or issues you need to address, the next step is to decide whether to engage, as my colleague Amy Edmondson has noted, in plan-then-implement change or promotion of collective learning.[5]

The straightforward plan-then-implement approach to change works well when you are sure that you have the following key supporting planks in place:

1. **Awareness:** A critical mass of people are aware of the need for change.

2. **Diagnosis:** You know what needs to be changed and why.

3. **Vision:** You have a compelling vision and a solid strategy.

4. **Plan:** You have the expertise to put together a detailed plan.

5. **Support:** You have a sufficiently powerful coalition to support implementation.

The plan-then-implement approach to change might work well in turnaround situations, for example, where people accept there is a problem, the fixes are more technical than cultural or political, and people are hungry for a solution.

If any of these five conditions are not met, however, the pure plan-then-implement approach to change can get you in trouble. If you are in a realignment, for example, and people are in denial about the need for change, they are likely to greet your plan with stony silence. You may therefore need to build awareness of the need for change, or sharpen the diagnosis of the problem, or create a compelling vision and strategy, or develop a solid cross-functional implementation plan, or create a coalition in support of change.

To accomplish any of these goals, you would be well advised to focus on setting up a collective learning process, and not on developing and imposing change plans. If many people in the organization are willfully blind to emerging problems, for example, you have to put in place a process to pierce through this veil. Rather than mount a frontal assault on the organization's defenses, you should engage in something akin to guerrilla warfare, slowly chipping at their resistance and raising their awareness of the need for change.

You can do this by exposing key people to new ways of operating and thinking about the business, such as new data on customer satisfaction and competitive offerings. Or you can do some benchmarking of best-in-class organizations, getting the group to analyze how your best competitors perform. Or you can bring people to envision new approaches to doing things, for example, by scheduling an off-site meeting to brainstorm about key objectives or about improving existing processes.

The key, then, is to figure out which parts of the change process can be best addressed through planning and which are better dealt with through collective learning. Think of a change that you want to make in your new organization. Now use the diagnostic flowchart in figure 4-2 to figure out where collective learning processes are likely to be important to your success.

### Getting Started on Behavior Change

As you plan to get early wins, remember that the means you use are as important as the ends you achieve. The initiatives you put in place to get early wins should do double duty by

FIGURE 4 - 2

## Diagnostic Framework for Managing Change

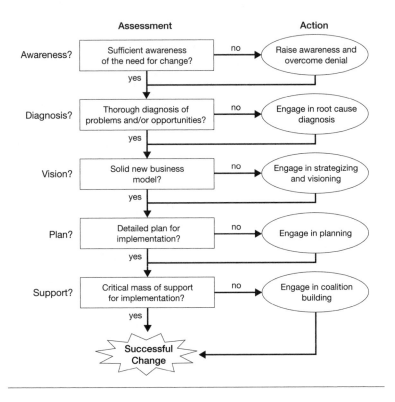

establishing new standards of behavior. Elena Lee did this when she carefully staffed and coached her project team and then quickly implemented their recommendations.

To change your organization, you will likely have to change its culture. This is a difficult undertaking. Your organization may have well-ingrained bad habits that you want to break. But we know how difficult it is for one person to change habitual patterns in any significant way, never mind a mutually reinforcing collection of people.

Simply blowing up the existing culture and starting over is rarely the right answer. People—and organizations—have limits on the change they can absorb all at once. And organizational cultures invariably have virtues as well as faults; they provide predictability and can be sources of pride. If you send the message that there is nothing good about the existing organization and its culture, you will rob people of a key source of stability in times of change. You also will deprive yourself of a potential wellspring of energy into which you could tap to improve performance.

The key is to identify both the good and bad elements of the existing culture. Elevate and praise the good elements even as you seek to change the bad. These functional aspects of the familiar culture are a bridge that can help carry people from the past to the future.

## Matching Strategy to Situation

The choice of behavior-change techniques should be a function of your group's structure, processes, skills, and—above all—its situation. Consider the difference between promoting behavior change in turnaround and realignment situations. In a turnaround, you face a combination of time pressure and the need to rapidly identify and secure the defendable core of the business. Techniques such as bringing in new people from the outside and setting up project teams to pursue specific performance-improvement initiatives often are a good fit. Contrast this with realignments, where you are well advised to start out with less obvious approaches to behavior change. By changing performance measures and starting benchmarking, for example, you set the stage for collective visioning about how to realign the business.

Finally, keep in mind your overarching goal: creating a virtuous cycle that reinforces wanted behavior and contributes to helping you achieve your A-item priorities. Remember that you are aiming at modest early improvements so you can pursue more fundamental changes.

## ACCELERATION CHECKLIST

1. Given your situation, what should be the timing and extent of each of the waves of change you envision?

2. Based on what you know now, what are your A-item priorities? Given these priorities, what do you need to do during your transition to lay the necessary groundwork for achieving them?

3. How would you like to see people behave differently by the end of your era in the organization? Describe as vividly as you can the behaviors you would like to encourage and discourage.

4. What can you begin to do to change behaviors during your transition?

5. How do you plan to connect yourself to your new organization? Who are your key audiences, and what messages would you like to convey to them? What are the best modes of engagement?

6. What are the most promising focal points for your early performance-improvement efforts? Select one focal point and think about how early wins in this area could serve as a model for how you want people to behave.

7. Given the changes you want to make, in what areas do you need to engage in collective learning?

# 5

# Negotiate Success

W HEN MICHAEL CHEN was promoted to manage the information technology (IT) function for a key business unit of an oil company, he was elated—until he received calls from two colleagues. Both told him the same thing: "Start updating your résumé. Cates is going to eat you alive."

His new boss, Vaughan Cates, was a hard-driving manager with a reputation for getting results—and for being tough on people. Cates had recently taken over the unit, and several of the people she had inherited had already left.

Michael's friends anticipated the problem. "You've had a lot of success," one said. "But Cates will think you're not aggressive enough. You're a planner and team builder. She'll think you're too slow and not up to the tough decisions."

Forewarned, Michael laid the groundwork with Cates to gain time for diagnosis and planning. "I want to operate on a 90-day time frame, starting with 30 days to get on top of things," he told her. "Then I will bring you a detailed assessment and plan with goals and actions for the next 60 days." Michael updated

Cates regularly on his progress. Pressed by her to make a call on a major systems purchase after three weeks, Michael held firm to his schedule. At the end of 30 days, he delivered a strong plan that pleased his new boss.

A month later, Michael returned to report some early wins and to ask Cates for more headcount to advance a key project. She subjected him to withering questioning, but he was on top of his business case. Eventually she agreed to his requests, but set some strict deadlines for achieving results. Armed with what he needed, Michael was soon able to report that he had met several interim targets.

Building on his momentum, Michael raised the question of style at their next meeting: "We have different styles, but I can deliver for you," he said. "I want you to judge me on my results, not on how I get them." It took nearly a year, but Michael built a solid, productive working relationship with Cates.

To succeed as Michael Chen did with a new boss, it is wise to *negotiate success* so you don't play a losing hand. It is well worth investing time in this critical relationship up front, because your new boss sets your benchmarks, interprets your actions for other key players, and controls access to resources you need. He or she will have more impact than any other individual on how quickly you reach the breakeven point, and on your eventual success or failure.

Negotiating success means proactively engaging with your new boss to shape the game so you have a fighting chance of achieving desired goals. Too many new leaders just play the game, reactively taking their situation as given and failing as a result. The alternative is to shape the game by negotiating with your boss to establish realistic expectations, reach consensus on the situation, and secure enough resources. By negotiating effectively with Vaughan Cates, Michael laid the foundation for his success.

Keep in mind that the nature of your relationship with your new boss should depend on your level in the organization and the business situation you face. The higher you rise, the more autonomy you are likely to get. This is especially the case if you and your boss are situated in different locations. Lack of oversight can be a blessing, if you get what you need to succeed, or it can be a curse, if you get enough rope to hang yourself.

What you need from a boss also varies among the various ST$_A$RS business situations. If you are in a realignment, you need your boss to help you make the case for change. In a sustaining-success situation, you will need help to learn about the business and avoid early mistakes that threaten the core assets. In start-ups, you need resources and protection from too much higher-level interference. In turnarounds, you may need to be pushed to cut back the business to the defendable core quickly.

There is much you can do to build a productive working relationship with your new boss. This chapter will show you how to engage in the right kinds of dialogue and how to create a 90-day plan. Read it even if you will be reporting to the same boss in your new role. Your relationship won't necessarily stay the same in a changed situation. The boss's expectations may be different, and you may need more resources. Many managers mistakenly assume that they can continue to work with a current boss in the same way despite a different role. Don't make this error.

Think also about how you might use the ideas in this chapter to accelerate relationship building with your own new direct reports. After all, don't you have a big stake in getting them to the breakeven point as quickly as possible?

## Focusing on the Fundamentals

When experienced managers are quizzed about how to build a productive relationship with a new boss, their observations typically emerge in the form of do's and don'ts. Let's start with the don'ts:

- **Don't trash the past.** There is nothing to be gained and much to be lost by criticizing the people who led the organization before you arrived. This doesn't mean that you should tolerate mediocrity. You need to understand the past, but concentrate on assessing current behavior and results, and on making the changes necessary to support improved performance.

- **Don't stay away.** If you have a boss who doesn't reach out to you, or with whom you have uncomfortable interactions, you will have to reach out yourself. Otherwise, you risk letting crippling communications or expectations gaps arise. It may feel good to be given a lot of rope, but resist the urge to take it. Get on your boss's calendar regularly. Be sure your boss is aware of the issues you face and that you are aware of the boss's expectations and whether and how they are shifting.

- **Don't surprise your boss.** It is no fun bringing your boss bad news. The danger that the messenger (you) will be shot is very real. However, most bosses consider it a far greater sin not to report emerging problems early enough. Worst of all is for your boss to learn about a problem from someone else. It is usually best to give your new boss at least a heads-up as soon as you become aware of a developing problem.

- **Don't approach your boss only with problems.** You don't want to be perceived as bringing nothing but problems for your boss to solve. You need to have a plan too. This emphatically does not mean that you have to fashion full-blown solutions: The outlay of time and effort needed to generate solutions can easily lure you down the rocky road to surprising your boss. The key here is to give just a few minutes' thought to how to address the problem, and to your role and the help you will need.

- **Don't run down your checklist.** There is a tendency, even for senior managers, to use meetings with a boss as an opportunity to run through your checklist of what you have been doing. There are times when this is appropriate, but it is rarely what your boss needs or wants to hear. As one senior executive put it, "I tell them [new direct reports] that I assume they are busy and that they should come to me to discuss what they are trying to do and how I can help them."

- **Don't try to change the boss.** One accomplished manager told a story about scheduling a midafternoon meeting with his boss and immediately launching into a review of an important issue, only to discover the boss was falling asleep. The manager had been surprised when making the appointment to find the midafternoon time slot open, not just that day but nearly every day. His peers had already figured out the boss needed a regular nap then and scheduled meetings at other hours. The point? Assume that you are not going to change your boss, and adapt to his or her style and idiosyncrasies.

There are some fundamental do's as well. If you follow them, life with your new boss will be easier:

- **Take 100 percent responsibility for making the relationship work.** This is the flip side of "Don't stay away." Don't expect your boss to reach out or to offer you the time and support you need. It is best to begin by assuming that it is on your shoulders to make the relationship work. If your boss meets you partway, it will be a welcome surprise.

- **Clarify mutual expectations early and often.** Begin managing expectations right away. You are in trouble if your boss expects you to fix things fast when you know the business has serious structural problems. It is wise to get bad news on the table early and to lower unrealistic expectations. Then check in regularly to make sure the boss's expectations have not shifted.

- **Negotiate timelines for diagnosis and action planning.** Don't let yourself get caught up immediately in fire-fighting, or pressured to make calls before you are ready. Buy yourself some time to diagnose the new organization and come up with an action plan. It worked for Michael Chen in his dealings with Vaughan Cates, and it can work for you. The 90-day plan discussed at the end of this chapter is an excellent vehicle for accomplishing this.

- **Aim for early wins in areas important to the boss.** Whatever your own priorities, figure out what the boss cares about most. What are his or her interests and goals, and how does what you are doing fit into this picture? Once you know, aim for early results in those areas.

One good way to do so is to focus on just three things that are important to your boss and to discuss what you are doing about them every time you interact. That way, your boss will feel some ownership of your success. But don't make the mistake of taking actions you think are misguided. In part, your job is to shape your boss's perceptions of what can and should be achieved.

- **Pursue good marks from those whose opinions your boss respects.** Your new boss's opinion of you will be based partly on direct interactions and partly on what he or she hears about you from trusted others. Your boss may have preexisting relationships with people who are now your subordinates. You needn't curry favor with the people your boss trusts. Simply be alert to the multiple channels through which information about you and your performance will reach your boss.

With these basic rules in mind, you can begin to plan how to engage with your new boss.

## Planning for Five Conversations

Your relationship with your new boss will be built through a continuing dialogue. Your discussions will begin before you accept the new position and continue into your transition and beyond. Several fundamental subjects belong at the center of this dialogue. In fact, it is valuable to include plans for five distinct "conversations" with your new boss about specific transition-related subjects in your 90-day plan. These are not subjects to be dealt with in separate appointments, but intertwined threads of dialogue.

1. **The situational diagnosis conversation.** In this conversation, you will seek to understand how your new boss sees the business situation. Is it a turnaround, a start-up, a realignment, or a sustaining-success situation? How did the organization reach this point? What factors—both soft and hard—make this situation a challenge? What resources within the organization can you draw on? Your view may differ from your boss's, but it is essential to grasp how he or she sees the situation.

2. **The expectations conversation.** Your agenda in this conversation will be to seek to understand and negotiate expectations. What does your new boss need you to do in the short term and in the medium term? What will constitute success? How will your performance be measured? When? You might conclude that your boss's expectations are unrealistic and that you need to work to reset them. Also, as part of your broader campaign to secure early wins, as discussed in chapter 4, keep in mind that it is better to under-promise and overdeliver.

3. **The style conversation.** This conversation is about how you and your new boss can best interact on an ongoing basis. What form of communication does he or she prefer? Face-to-face? In writing? By voicemail or e-mail? How often? What kinds of decisions does he or she want to be consulted on and when can you make the call on your own? How do your styles differ and what are the implications of your differences for how you should interact?

4. **The resources conversation.** This conversation is essentially a negotiation for critical resources. What is it that you will need to be successful? What do you need your boss to do? The resources in question need not be limited to funding or personnel. In a realignment, for example, you may need help from your boss to persuade the organization to confront the need for change.

5. **The personal development conversation.** Finally, discuss how your tenure in this job will contribute to your personal development. In what areas do you need improvement? Are there projects or special assignments you could undertake (without sacrificing focus)? Are there courses or programs that would strengthen your capabilities?

In practice, your dialogue about these subjects will mingle threads and evolve over time. You might address several of the five issues in a single meeting, or you might work out issues related to one subject through a series of brief exchanges. Michael Chen covered style and expectations in a single meeting and established a schedule for talking about the situation and more deeply about expectations.

There is a logic to the sequence just described, however. Your early conversations should focus on situational diagnosis, expectations, and style. As you learn more, you will be ready to negotiate for resources, revisiting your diagnosis of the situation and resetting expectations as necessary. When you feel the relationship is reasonably well established, you can introduce the personal development conversation. Take some time to plan for each conversation, and signal clearly to your boss what you hope to accomplish in each exchange.

The detailed guidelines that follow will help you plan each of the five conversations with your new boss.

## Planning the Situation Conversation

Reaching a shared understanding of the business situation you face, and of its associated challenges and opportunities, is your goal in the *situational diagnosis conversation*. This shared understanding is the foundation for everything you will do. If you and your boss do not define your new situation in the same way, you will not receive the support you need to achieve your objectives. Thus, your first discussion with your new boss should center on clearly defining your new situation using the $ST_ARS$ model as a shared language.

### Match Support to Your Situation

The support you need from your boss will depend on the scenario—whether it is a start-up, turnaround, realignment, or sustaining-success situation. Once you reach a common understanding of the situation, think carefully about the role you would like your new boss to play and what kinds of support you will ask for. In all four situations, you will need your boss to give you the direction, support, and space to do *your* job. Table 5-1 lists typical roles your boss might play in each of the $ST_ARS$ situations.

## Planning the Expectations Conversation

The point of the *expectations conversation* is for you and your boss to clarify and align your expectations about the future. You

**TABLE 5-1**

## Matching Support to Your Situation

| Situation | Typical Roles for Your Boss |
|---|---|
| Start-up | • Help getting needed resources quickly<br>• Clear, measurable goals<br>• Guidance at strategic breakpoints<br>• Help staying focused |
| Turnaround | Same as start-up, plus<br><br>• Support for making and implementing tough personnel calls<br>• Support for changing or correcting the external image of the organization and its people<br>• Help cutting deeply enough and early enough |
| Realignment | Same as start-up, plus<br><br>• Help making the case for change, especially if you are coming in from outside the organization |
| Sustaining success | • Constant reality testing: Is this a sustaining-success situation or is it a realignment?<br>• Support for playing good defense and avoiding mistakes that damage the business<br>• Help finding ways to take the business to a new level |

need to agree on short- and medium-term goals, on timing, and on how your boss will measure progress. What will constitute success, for your boss and for you? When does your boss expect to see results? How will you measure success? Over what time frame? If you succeed, what is next? If you don't manage expectations, they will manage you.

### Match Expectations to the Situation

Closely align your expectations with your shared assessment of the situation. In a turnaround situation, for example, you and your boss would probably agree on the need to take decisive action quickly. You would both have explicit expectations for the immediate future, such as making difficult decisions to reduce costs in nonessential areas or concentrating on the products with the highest margins. In this scenario, you would probably measure success by improvements in the business's overall financial performance.

### Aim for Early Wins in Areas Important to Your Boss

Whatever your own priorities, pinpoint what your boss cares about most and aim for some early wins in those areas. If you want to succeed, you need your boss's help; in turn, you should help your boss succeed. When you pay attention to your boss's priorities, he or she will feel ownership in your success. The most effective and synergistic approach is to integrate your boss's goals with your own efforts to get early wins. If this is impossible, look for some early wins based solely on your boss's priorities.

### Identify the "Untouchables"

If there are parts of the organization—products, facilities, people—about which your new boss is proprietary, it is essential to figure out what they are as soon as possible. You don't want to find out that you are pressing to shut down the product line that your boss started up or to replace someone who has been his or her loyal ally. So try to deduce what your boss is sensitive about. You can do this by understanding your boss's personal history, by talking to others, and by paying close attention to facial expression, tone, and body language. If you are uncertain, float an idea gently as a trial balloon and then watch the boss's reactions closely.

### Educate Your Boss

One of your immediate tasks is to shape your boss's perceptions of what you can and should achieve. You may find your boss's expectations unrealistic, or simply at odds with your own beliefs about what needs to be done. If so, you will have to work hard to make your views converge. In a realignment situation, for example, your boss may attribute the worst problems to a certain part of the business, whereas you believe they lie elsewhere. In this case, you will need to educate your boss about the underlying problems to reset expectations. Proceed carefully—especially if your boss feels invested in the way things have always been or is partially responsible for the problems.

### Underpromise and Overdeliver

Whether you and your boss agree on expectations, try to bias yourself somewhat toward underpromising achievements and overdelivering results. This strategy contributes to building credibility. Consider how your organization's capacity for change might affect your ability to deliver on the promises you make. Be conservative in what you promise. If you deliver more, you will delight your boss. But if you promise too much and fail to deliver, you risk undermining your credibility. Even if you do a great deal, you will have failed in the boss's eyes.

### Clarify, Clarify, Clarify

Even if you are sure you know what your boss expects, you should go back regularly to confirm and clarify. Some bosses know what they want but are not good at expressing it; you could reach clarity only after you have headed down the wrong road.

So you have to be prepared to keep asking questions until you are sure you understand. Try, for example, asking the same questions in different ways to gain more insight. Work at reading between the lines accurately and developing good hypotheses about what your boss is likely to want. Try to put yourself in your boss's shoes and understand how his or her boss will evaluate him or her. Figure out how you fit into the larger picture. Above all, don't let key issues remain ambiguous. Ambiguity about goals and expectations is dangerous. As one new leader put it, "A tie [in a conflict over what was said about expectations in an earlier conversation] doesn't go to you, it goes to your supervisor."

### Working with Multiple Bosses

You face even more daunting challenges in managing expectations if you have more than one boss or are situated in a different location from your boss. The same fundamental principles hold, but the relative emphasis shifts. If you have multiple bosses, you have to be sure to balance perceived wins and losses among them carefully. If one boss has substantially more power, then it makes sense to bias yourself somewhat in his or her direction early on, so long as you redress the balance, to the greatest extent possible, later. If you can't get agreement by working with your bosses one-on-one, you have to essentially force them to come to the table together to thrash issues out. Otherwise, you will get pulled to pieces.

### Working at a Distance

Managing when you are located far from your boss presents a different set of challenges. The risk of falling out of step without realizing it is naturally greater. This puts the onus on you to exert even more discipline over communication, scheduling calls and meetings to be sure that you stay aligned. It also is even more critical to establish clear and comprehensive metrics so that your boss gets a reasonable picture of what is going on, and you can manage effectively by exception.

## Planning the Style Conversation

People's stylistic preferences affect how they learn, communicate, influence others, and make decisions. In the *style conversation,* your agenda will be to determine how you and your boss can best work together on a continuing basis. This was the key challenge that Michael Chen faced in working out his relationship with Vaughan Cates. Even if your boss never becomes a close friend or mentor, it is essential that he or she respect your professional capabilities.

### Diagnose Your Boss's Style

The first step is to diagnose your new boss's working style and to figure out how it jibes with your own. If you leave voicemail messages for her about an urgent problem and she doesn't respond quickly, but then reproaches you for not giving her a heads-up about the problem, take note: Your boss doesn't use voicemail!

How does your boss like to communicate? How often? What kinds of decisions does your boss want to be involved in, and when can you make calls on your own? Does your boss arrive at the office early and work late? Does he or she expect others to do the same?

Pinpoint the specific ways in which your styles differ and what those differences imply about how you will interact. Suppose you prefer to learn by talking with knowledgeable people, whereas your boss relies more on reading and analyzing hard data. What kinds of misunderstandings and problems might this stylistic difference cause and how can you avoid them? Or suppose your new boss tends to micromanage while you prefer a lot of independence. What can you do to manage this tension?

You may find it helpful to talk to others who have worked with your boss in the past. Naturally, you have to do this judiciously. Be careful not to be perceived as eliciting criticism of how the boss manages. Stick to less fraught issues, such as how the boss prefers to communicate. Listen to others' perspectives, but base your evolving strategy chiefly on your own experience.

Observe too how your boss deals with others. Is there consistency? If not, why not? Does the boss have favorites? Is he particularly prone to micromanaging certain issues? Has he come down hard on a few people because of unacceptable performance?

### Scope Out the Dimensions of Your Box

Your boss will have a comfort zone about involvement in decision making. Think of this zone as defining the boundaries of the decision-making "box" in which you will operate. What sorts of decisions does your boss want you to make on your own but tell her about? Are you free, for example, to make key personnel decisions? When does she want to be consulted before you decide? Is it when your actions touch on broader issues of policy—for example, in granting people leave? Or when there are hot political issues associated with some of the projects you are working on? When does she want to make the decision herself?

Initially, expect to be confined to a relatively small box. As your new boss gains confidence in you, the dimensions of the box should increase. If not, or if it remains too small to allow you to be effective, you may have to address the issue directly.

### Adapt to Your Boss's Style

Assume that the job of building a positive relationship with your new boss is 100 percent your responsibility. In short, this means adapting to his or her style. If your boss hates voicemail, don't use it. If he or she wants to know in detail what is going on, overcommunicate. Do not do anything that could compromise your ability to achieve superior business results, but do look for opportunities to smooth the day-to-day workings of your relationship. Others who have worked with your boss can tell you what approaches they found successful. Then judiciously experiment with the tactics that seem most promising in your case. When in doubt, simply ask your boss how he or she would prefer you to proceed.

### Address the Difficult Issues

When serious style differences arise, it is best to address them directly. Otherwise, you run the risk that your boss will interpret a style difference as disrespect or even incompetence on your part. Raise the style issue before it becomes a source of irritation, and talk with your boss about how to accommodate both your styles. This conversation can smooth the path for both of you to achieve your goals.

One proven strategy is to focus your early conversations on goals and results, instead of how you achieve them. You might simply say that you expect to notice differences in how the two of you approach certain issues or decisions, but that you are completely committed to achieving the results to which you have both agreed. An assertion of this kind prepares your boss to expect differences. You may have to remind your boss periodically to focus on the results you are achieving, not on your methods.

It may also help to judiciously discuss style issues with someone your boss trusts, who can enlighten you about potential issues and solutions before you raise them directly with your boss. If you find the right adviser, he or she may even help you broach a difficult issue in a nonthreatening manner.

Don't make the mistake of trying to address all style issues in a single conversation. Nevertheless, a dialogue explicitly devoted to style is an excellent place to start. Expect to continue to be attentive to, and adapt to, the boss's style as your relationship evolves.

## Planning the Resources Conversation

The *resources conversation* is an ongoing negotiation with your new boss for critical resources. Before you launch this conversation, you should agree with your boss on the business situation you face, goals and expectations, and mutually effective working styles. Now you must secure the resources you need to meet expectations.

The resources you need will depend on the situation and differ at different points in time.

- In a *start-up situation,* your most urgent needs are likely to be adequate financial resources, technical support, and people with the right expertise.

- In a *turnaround situation,* you need authority, backed by political support, to make the tough decisions and secure scarce financial and human resources.

- In a *realignment situation,* you need consistent, public backing to get the organization to confront the need for change. Ideally, your boss will stand shoulder to shoulder with you, helping to pierce through denial and complacency.

- In a *sustaining-success situation,* you require financial and technical resources to sustain the core business and exploit promising new opportunities. You also need periodic pushes to set stretch goals that will keep you from drifting into complacency.

The first step is to decide what resources—tangible and intangible—you must have to succeed. Identify the resources already available to you, such as experienced people or new products ready to be launched. Then identify the resources you will need help in obtaining. Ask yourself: "What exactly do I need from my boss?" The sooner you can articulate the resources you need, the sooner you can broach these requests in conversations with your boss.

It is best to put as much as possible on the table as early as possible. Try using the "menu" approach, by laying out the costs and benefits of different levels of resource commitment. "If you want my sales to grow 7 percent next year, I need investment of $x. If you want 10 percent growth, I will need $y." Going back to the well too often is a sure way to lose credibility. If it takes some more time to get a handle on what resources you need to achieve specific goals, then so be it. Michael Chen negotiated for the necessary time—a critical resource—so he could avoid this problem.

**Play or Change the Game?**

You may be able to achieve your goals by playing the game according to the prevailing rules. If you can maneuver within the accepted cultural and political norms, your resource requests will be expected—and you will find it easier to get what you need.

In other situations—notably realignments and turnarounds—you may need to change or even abandon established ways of doing business. Your resource requests will probably be more sweeping, and failure to secure them more damaging. You will have to negotiate harder to get what you need. These circumstances call for being clear about how the situation, expectations, and resources all have to line up to give you a reasonable shot at success. Clarify your needs in your own mind before you enter these discussions, back them up with as much hard data as you can get, and prepare to explain exactly why you see certain resources as essential. Then stick to your guns. Keep coming back. Enlist others to help make your case. Seek out allies within and outside your organization. It is better to push too hard than to slowly bleed to death.

**Negotiate for Resources**

As you seek commitments for resources, keep these principles of effective negotiation in mind:

- **Focus on underlying interests.** Probe as deeply as possible to understand the agendas of your boss and any others from whom you need to secure resources. What is in it for them?

- **Look for mutually beneficial exchanges.** Seek resources that both support your boss's agenda and advance your own. Look for ways to help peers advance their agendas in return for help with yours.

- **Link resources to results.** Highlight the performance benefits that will result if more resources are dedicated to your unit. Create a "menu" laying out what you can achieve (and not achieve) with current resources and what different-sized increments would allow you to do.

## Planning the Personal Development Conversation

Finally, when your relationship with your boss has matured a bit, begin to discuss how your tenure in this position will contribute to your personal development. What skills do you need to develop to do the job better? Are there shortcomings in your management capacities that you need to try to address? Are there projects or special assignments that you could get involved in (without sacrificing focus) that could strengthen your skills? Are there formal courses or programs that would strengthen your capabilities?

It is especially critical that you do this when you are making key career passages. If you are a first-time manager, get in the habit early of asking your boss for feedback and help in developing your supervisory skills. Your willingness to seek candid feedback on your strengths and weaknesses and, critically, your ability to act on the feedback send a powerful message.

The same fundamental principle holds whether you are becoming a manager of managers for the first time, a functional leader, a general manager, or a CEO. Whenever you are at a point in your career when success demands a different set of skills and attitudes, discipline yourself to be open to learning from others who have gone before you.

Don't restrict your focus to hard skills. The higher you rise, the more important the key soft skills of cultural and political diagnosis, negotiation, coalition building, and conflict management will become. Formal training can help, but developmental assignments—in project teams, in new parts of the organization, in different functions, in different locations—are indispensable in honing these key managerial skills.

## Putting It All Together: Your 90-Day Plan

No matter what type of situation you are entering, it can be useful to put together a 90-day plan and to get buy-in from your boss. Usually, you will be able to devise a plan after a couple of weeks in the new job, when you have begun to connect with the organization and to get the lay of the land.

Your 90-day plan should be written, even if it just consists of bullet points. It should specify priorities and goals as well as milestones. Critically, you should share it with your boss and seek buy-in for it. It should serve as a "contract" between the two of you about how you are going to spend your time, spelling out both what you will do and what you will not do.

To begin to develop your plan, divide the 90 days into three blocks of 30 days. At the end of each block, you will have a review meeting with your boss. (Naturally, you are likely to interact more often than that.) You should typically devote the first block of 30 days to learning and building personal credibility. Like Michael Chen, you should negotiate for this early learning period and then try to hold your boss to that agreement. Then you can proceed to develop a learning agenda and learning plan for yourself. Set weekly goals for yourself and establish a personal discipline of weekly evaluation and planning.

Your key outputs at the end of the first 30 days will be a diagnosis of the situation, identification of key priorities, and a plan for how you will spend the next 30 days. This plan should address where and how you will begin to seek some early wins. Your review meeting with your boss should focus on the situation and expectations conversations, with an eye to reaching consensus about the situation, clarification of expectations, and buy-in to your plan for the next 30 days. Continue the weekly discipline of evaluation and planning.

At the 60-day mark, your review meeting should focus on assessing your progress toward the goals of your plan for the previous 30 days. You should also discuss what you plan to achieve in the next 30 days (that is, by the end of 90 days). Depending on the situation and your level in the organization, your goals at this juncture might include identifying the resources necessary to pursue major initiatives, fleshing out your initial assessments of strategy and structure, and presenting some early assessments of your team.

## Developing Yourself as a Boss

Finally, you won't merely *have* a new boss; you are likely to *be* a new boss as well. You will almost certainly have new subordinates. Just as you need to develop a productive relationship with your new boss, so too they need to work effectively with you. In the past, have you done a good job of helping subordinates make their own transitions? What might you do differently this time?

Think about how to apply all the advice in this chapter to working with your own direct reports. The golden rule of transitions is to transition others as you would wish to be transitioned yourself (see "The Golden Rule of Transitions"). The same five-conversation framework can help to build productive relationships with the people who report to you. Introduce the framework to them right away and schedule a first conversation with each of them to talk about the situation and about your expectations. Get them to do some prework before the meeting—for example, reading chapter 3 on matching strategy to situation. See how fast you can accelerate their transitions.

Finally, seek to learn from bad bosses as well as good ones. You will inevitably experience a less-than-stellar boss at some

---

### The Golden Rule of Transitions

Think about how you would like new bosses to help you transition into new roles. Ideally, what kinds of guidance and support would they give you? Now think about how you deal with new direct reports. What kinds of guidance and support do you give them? Now juxtapose these assessments. Do you transition others as you would wish to be transitioned yourself? If there is a big inconsistency between how you would prefer to be dealt with as a new direct report and how you deal with new direct reports, then you are part of the problem.

Helping direct reports to accelerate their transitions is about more than being a good manager and contributing to others' development. The faster your direct reports get up to speed, the better able they will be to help you reach your goals.

---

point in your career. A surprising number of managers remark that "I've learned more from my bad bosses than my good ones." Bad bosses forced them to think about the negative impact of a bad boss. If you find yourself suffering under a bad boss, take the time to figure out his or her faults and what good bosses do differently, and then apply those insights to yourself.

### ACCELERATION CHECKLIST

1. How effectively have you built relationships with new bosses in the past? What have you done well? In what areas do you need improvement?

2. Create a plan for the situational diagnosis conversation. Based on what you know now, what issues will you raise with your boss in this conversation? What do you want to say up front? In what order do you want to raise issues?

3. Create a plan for the expectations conversation. How will you figure out what your new boss expects you to do?

4. Create a plan for the style conversation. How will you figure out how your boss prefers to interact with you? What mode of communication (e-mail, voicemail, face-to-face) does he or she prefer? How often should you interact? How much detail should you provide? What types of issues should you consult with him or her about before deciding?

5. Create a plan for the resources conversation. Given what you need to do, what resources are absolutely

needed? With fewer resources, what would you have to forgo? If you had more resources, what would the benefits be? Be sure to build the business case!

6. Create a plan for the personal development conversation. What are your strengths and where do you need improvement? What kinds of assignments or projects might help you develop skills you need?

# 6

# Achieve Alignment

HANNAH JAFFEY, a former human resources consultant, took a position as vice president of human resources at an investment services company. The organization was suffering from such intense internal conflict that some senior executives were barely on speaking terms. Hannah's job was to support the president in making personnel changes—and to turn the situation around.

Hannah soon realized the company's structure and incentives system needed overhauling as well. As the company had grown, senior management had organized new products into separate business units. With recent market changes, several units' customer bases overlapped, yet the units had no incentives to cooperate. The result? Confused customers and conflicts over which units "owned" key customer relationships.

Convinced the company needed structural realignment, Hannah approached her new boss, the president of the company. She laid out her case, but he remained convinced the people were the problem. The organizational structure had worked well in the past, he told Hannah, and with the right people in place it would work again.

But Hannah kept coming back to him on the issue. She brought to his attention situations in which incentive misalignments were unnecessarily stoking conflict. She also collected data on how other companies had organized to deal with similar issues. It took some time, but eventually Hannah convinced the president that the firm needed structural changes as well as personnel changes.

The company shifted the focus of its marketing and sales units from products to customers, and consolidated operations into a single group that supported all units. At the same time, the president brought in a new head of sales. The realignment worked: A year later, the company was functioning smoothly, customers were much happier, and profits were up 15 percent.

The higher you climb in organizations, the more you take on the role of organizational architect, creating the context within which others can achieve superior performance. No matter how charismatic you are, you cannot hope to do much if the key elements in your unit are fundamentally out of alignment. You will feel like you are pushing a boulder uphill every day.

If strategy, structure, systems, and skills are within your purview in your new position, you need to begin to analyze the architecture of your organization and assess alignment among these key elements. You can't hope to do much more than conduct a solid diagnosis and perhaps get started on addressing alignment issues in the first few months. But plans to assess the architecture of your group and to begin identifying areas for improvement should be included in your 90-day plan.

Armed with the resulting insights, you can begin to take actions during your transition to align strategy, structure, systems, and skills, thus making superior performance possible. Naturally, this is not something that you can complete in a few months. But it is essential that you get started on fixing the worst realignments. In fact, this may be a key way you create value and reach the breakeven point in your organization.

Even if, like Hannah Jaffey, you lack the authority to alter your new organization single-handedly, you should still read this chapter. You may need to convince influential people— your boss or your peers—that serious misalignments are a key impediment to achieving superior performance. Also, a thorough understanding of organizational alignment can help you build credibility with people higher in the organization—and demonstrate your potential for more senior positions.

## Designing Organizational Architecture

Begin by thinking of yourself as the architect of your unit or group. This may be a familiar role for you, but it probably isn't. Few managers get systematic training in organizational design. Because managers typically have limited control over organizational design early in their careers, they learn little about it. It is commonplace for less-senior people to complain about misalignments and to wonder aloud why "those idiots" higher up let obviously dysfunctional arrangements continue. By the time you reach the mid-senior levels of most organizations, however, you are well on your way to becoming one of those idiots. You are therefore well advised to begin learning something about how to assess and design organizations.

To equip your group to achieve its goals, five elements of organizational architecture all need to work together:[1]

- **Strategy:** The core approach the organization will use to accomplish its goals

- **Structure:** How people are situated in units and how their work is coordinated

- **Systems:**  The processes used to add value

- **Skills:**  The capabilities of the various groups of people in the organization

- **Culture:**  The values, norms, and assumptions that shape behavior

Certainly, you need a focused strategy to move forward effectively. But misalignments among *any* of these five elements can make even the best strategy useless. Strategy drives the other elements *and* is influenced by them. For example, if you decide to change your group's strategy, you will probably have to alter its structure, systems, and skills to support the new plan. As figure 6-1 shows, clarifying your strategy and aligning the supporting elements have to go hand in hand.

**FIGURE 6 - 1**

## Elements of Organizational Architecture

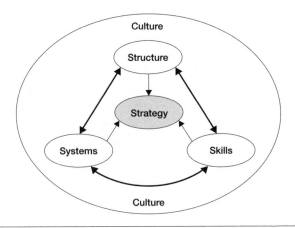

# Identifying Misalignments

Organizations can end up misaligned in many ways. Your goal during your first 90 days should be to identify potential misalignments and then design a plan for correcting them. Common types of misalignment include the following:

- **Skills and strategy misalignment.** Suppose you head an R&D group and your goal is to increase the number of new product ideas your team generates. However, your group does not understand the latest techniques and support tools that would let you run more experiments faster than before. In this case, your group's skills do not support its strategy.

- **Systems and strategy misalignment.** Imagine that you lead a marketing group whose strategy is to focus on a new customer segment. If the group has not established an effective way to compile and analyze information about those customers, your group's systems fail to support its strategy.

- **Structure and systems misalignment.** Suppose you manage a product development group whose members are organized by product line. The rationale for this structure is that it focuses specialized technical expertise on specific products. But this structure has a downside: The group does not have efficient systems for integrating the overlapping expertise of different product teams. The resulting mismatch between structure and systems would make it difficult for the entire group to perform optimally.

## Avoiding Some Common Traps

Too many managers rely on simplistic fixes to address compli-
cated alignment problems. Be alert to these all-too-common
pitfalls:

- **Trying to restructure your way out of deeper problems.**
  Overhauling your group's structure in times of trouble
  can amount to straightening the deck chairs on the
  *Titanic.* Resist doing so until you understand whether
  restructuring will address the root causes of the
  problems. Otherwise, you may create new misalignments and have to backtrack, disrupting your
  group, lowering productivity, and damaging your
  credibility.

- **Creating structures that are too complex.** This is a
  related trap. Although it may look good on paper to
  create a structure, such as a matrix, in which people in
  different units share accountability and in which "creative tensions" get worked out through their interactions, too often the result is bureaucratic paralysis.
  Strive where possible for clear lines of accountability.
  Simplify the structure to the greatest degree possible
  without compromising core goals.

- **Automating problem processes.** Automating your
  group's core processes may produce significant gains
  in productivity, quality, and reliability, but it is a mistake to simply speed up an existing process through
  technology if the process has serious underlying problems. Automation will not solve such problems and
  may even amplify them. Analyze and streamline

processes first; then decide whether automating them still makes sense.

- **Making changes for change's sake.** Resist the temptation to tear down the fences before you know why they were put up. New leaders who feel self-imposed pressure to put their stamp on the organization often make changes in strategy or structure before they really understand the business. Here again, the action imperative discussed in chapter 2 creates a sure recipe for disaster.

- **Overestimating your group's capacity to absorb strategic shifts.** It is easy to envision an ambitious new strategy. In practice, though, it is difficult for a group to change in response to large-scale strategic shifts. Advance incrementally if time allows. Focus on a vital few priorities. Make modest changes to your group's strategy; experiment; and then progressively refine structure, processes, skills, and culture.

## Getting Started

Aligning an organization is like preparing for a long sailing trip. First you select your destination (the mission and goals) and your route (the strategy). Then you figure out what boat you need (the structure), how to outfit it (the systems), and the crew mix (the skills). Throughout the journey, you keep an eye out for reefs that are not on the charts.

The underlying point is that there is a logic to organizational alignment. Changing the structure before figuring out the strategy is unlikely to be productive. Also, you cannot assess the fitness of your existing crew until you have a handle on your destination, route, and boat.

1. **Start with strategy.** Begin by taking a hard look at how your unit is positioned with respect to the larger organization's goals and your A-item priorities. Make sure your strategy is well thought through and logically integrated.

2. **Look at supporting structure, systems, and skills.** Next, look at whether your group's existing structure, systems, and skills will support the changes in strategy you envision. Dig into and understand these capabilities. If one or more of them is ill-suited to the strategy you have in mind, figure out how you will adapt your strategy and build (or acquire) the capabilities you need.

3. **Decide how and when you will introduce the new strategy.** Armed with a deeper understanding of your group's current capabilities, chart a path for shifting strategy (if such a shift is necessary). Block out both changes in positioning (markets, customers, and suppliers) and changes in supporting capabilities. Then adopt a realistic time frame for making these changes.

4. **Reshape structure, systems, and skills simultaneously.** There is little point in reshaping your group's structure until you have worked out the implications of doing so for systems and for the supporting skills of your group. Avoid the temptation to deal with structure and systems in isolation; they are tightly linked.

5. **Close the loop.** As you learn more about your group's structure, systems, and skills, you will gain insight into

the team's capabilities and its cultural capacity for change. This insight will in turn deepen your understanding of what changes in strategic positioning are possible over what time period.

## Crafting Strategy

A well-thought-out and logical strategy will enable your group to accomplish its objectives and contribute to the larger organization's competitive edge. A strategy defines what your organization will do and, critically, what it won't do.

The fundamental strategic questions concern customers, capital, capabilities, and commitments. Use the following list to quickly sketch out your unit's strategy.

- **Customers.** Which set of existing customers will we continue to serve? Which markets are we going to exit? What new markets are we going to enter, and when are we going to do it?

- **Capital.** Of the businesses we will remain in, which will we invest in and which will we draw cash from? What additional capital is likely to be required and when? Where will it come from?

- **Capabilities.** What are we good at and not good at? What existing organizational capabilities (for example, a strong new-product development organization) can we leverage? Which do we need to build up? Which do we need to create or acquire?

- **Commitments.** What critical resource commitment decisions do we need to make? When? What difficult-to-reverse past commitments do we have to live with or try to unwind?

It is beyond the scope of this book to delve deeply into business strategy, but excellent resources are available to help you answer these questions. (See the suggestions in the Recommended Reading section at the end of the book.) Our focus here is on assessing strategy by looking at its coherence, adequacy, and implementation.

### Assessing Coherence

Does a logic underlie the market segment choices, products, technologies, plans, and goals that compose the strategy? Assessing whether the elements of a strategy fit together calls for looking at the logic behind it to ensure that it makes sense overall. Have the people who developed the strategy thought through all its ramifications and the practical aspects of implementing it?

How do you evaluate a strategy's logic? Start by looking at documents that describe your group's strategy, such as strategic plans and mission statements. Then disassemble the strategy into its components—markets, products, technologies, functional plans, and goals. Ask yourself: Do the various dimensions of the strategy support one another? Is there a logical thread connecting these various parts? To be more specific, is there an obvious connection between market analysis and the group's objectives? Does the product-development budget jibe with the capital investments projected in the operations part of the strategy? Are plans in place to prepare salespeople for new products in the pipeline?

If the strategy makes sense overall, you will spot such connections easily.

### Assessing Adequacy

Is the strategy sufficient for what the group needs to do in the next two to three years? Will the strategy help your group support the larger organization's goals? Your group's strategy may be well thought through and logically integrated. But is it also adequate? That is, will it empower the group to carry out what it needs to do to succeed—and to help the larger organization succeed—in the next two to three years?

To assess adequacy, use these three approaches:

1. **Ask some probing questions.** Does your boss believe the strategy will provide enough return on the effort your group will expend to implement it? Are there plans in place to secure, develop, and preserve resources with which to carry out the strategy? Are profit and other targets high enough to keep the group on the right track? Is enough money earmarked for capital investment? For research?

2. **Use the well-known SWOT method: Analyze the strengths, weaknesses, opportunities, and threats associated with the strategy.**[2] Here's an example of each:

   - A strategy strength: Flexibility to develop and launch new products in response to rapid changes in customer preferences

   - A strategy weakness: Overreliance on a few aging products

   - A strategy opportunity: A new market that your group might serve by extending an existing brand

   - A strategy threat: A competitor that is entering a core market with a superior new technology

3. **Probe the history of the strategy's creation.** Find out who drove the strategy development process. Did they rush the process? Drag it out? If the former, they might not have thought through all the ramifications. If the latter, it might represent a lowest-common-denominator compromise that emerged from a political battle. Any mistakes during the development process could compromise the strategy's adequacy.

### Assessing Implementation

Has the strategy been implemented energetically? If not, why not? Next, look at how your group's strategy is being implemented—what people are *doing*, not what they are saying. Doing so will help you pinpoint whether problems stem from inadequacies in strategy *formulation* or strategy *implementation*. Ask yourself these kinds of questions:

- Are the performance metrics specified in the strategy used to make day-to-day decisions?

- Are the performance aspects that management actually uses consistent with the strategy's emphasis? What goals does the organization seem to be pursuing?

- If the strategy requires teamwork and cross-functional integration, are people acting as teams and collaborating across functions?

- If the strategy requires new employee skills, is a training-and-development infrastructure in place to develop those skills?

Your answers to these kinds of questions will tell you whether to push for changes in your group's stated strategy or in its implementation of the strategy.

## Modifying Strategy

Suppose you discover serious flaws in the strategy you have inherited. Can you radically change the strategy or the way it is implemented? That depends on two factors: the $ST_ARS$ situation you are entering, and your ability to persuade others and build support for your ideas.

Proposing significant changes to strategy is most difficult in realignments. You have to convince people who believe that their unit or team is already performing well using existing approaches. If you believe that the strategy has put the group on the wrong path, your main job will be to raise questions to persuade your boss and others to reexamine the strategy. You can ask questions such as the following:

- If we were to achieve this plan, what might some of the *unintended* results be?

- I see this plan as aimed at serving a broader market. Is that what we want?

- This plan is aggressive. What other goals will we need to put on hold to achieve it?

If you conclude that the existing strategy will move the group forward, but neither fast enough nor far enough, the wisest course may be to tweak it early on and plan for bigger changes later. For example, you might raise the targeted revenue goals modestly, or recommend investing in a needed technology sooner than the strategy calls for. More fundamental changes should wait until you've learned more and built support among key constituencies.

## Shaping Your Group's Structure

Once you have clarified what changes your group's strategy needs, you can address structural changes to support the desired strategy.

What is structure exactly? Most simply, your group's structure is the way it organizes people and technology to support its strategy.[3] Structure consists of the following elements:

- **Units:** How your direct reports are grouped, such as by function, product, or geographical area.

- **Decision rights:** Who is empowered to make what kinds of decisions and how.

- **Performance measurement and reward systems:** What performance-evaluation metrics and reward systems are in place.

- **Reporting relationships and information-sharing mechanisms:** How people observe and control the way work gets done, and how they share information and make high-level decisions.

### Assessing Structure

Before you begin to generate ideas for reshaping your group's structure, look into how the four structural elements interact. Are the pieces out of tune or in harmony? Ask yourself:

- Does the way team members are grouped help us achieve our strategic goals? Are the right people in the right places to work toward our core objectives?

- Is our decision-making structure letting us make the best decisions efficiently?

- Are we measuring and rewarding the kinds of achievements that matter most to our strategic aims?

- Do our reporting relationships promote sharing the right information at the right time and monitoring work in a way that supports our strategy?

If you are in a start-up situation—and therefore forming a new group—you will not have existing structures to evaluate. Instead, think about how you *want* the structural pieces to work in your group.

### Grappling with the Trade-offs

There is no perfect organization; every one embodies trade-offs. Thus, your challenge is to find the right balance for *your* situation. As you consider changes in your group's structure, keep in mind some all-too-common problems that can arise:

- **The team's knowledge base is too narrow or broad.**
  When you group people with *similar* experience and capabilities, they can accumulate deep wells of expertise. But if their knowledge base becomes too narrow and specialized, isolation and compartmentalization can result. Groups with a *broad mix* of skills may be able to integrate their knowledge more successfully, though at the cost of developing deeper expertise.

- **Employees' decision-making scope is too narrow or broad.** A good general rule is that decisions should be made by the people who have the most relevant knowledge, so long as their incentives encourage them to do what is best for the organization. If your group's decision-making process is centralized, you (and perhaps several other individuals) can decide quickly. But you may be forgoing the benefit of the wisdom of others who are better equipped to make certain of those decisions. This structure can lead to ill-informed decisions and can tax those who make all the decisions. If, on the other hand, people are given decision-making scope but do not understand the larger implications of their choices, they may make unwise calls.

- **Employees are inappropriately rewarded.** Effective managers align the interests of each decision maker with the interests of the group as a whole. This is why team-based reward systems are effective in some organizations: They focus everyone's attention on the group's ability to work together. Problems arise when measurement and compensation schemes fail to reward employees for either their individual *or* their collective efforts. Problems also arise when rewards advance employees' individual interests at the expense of the group's broader goals—such as when multiple employees who could serve the same set of customers lack incentives to cooperate. This was the problem confronting Hannah Jaffey at the beginning of the chapter.

- **Reporting relationships lead to compartmentalization or diffusion of accountability.** Reporting relationships help you observe and control the workings of your group, clarify responsibility, and encourage accountability. Hierarchical reporting relationships make these tasks easier but can lead to compartmentalization and poor information sharing. More complex reporting arrangements, such as matrix structures, broaden information sharing and reduce compartmentalization but can dangerously diffuse accountability.

## Aligning Key Systems

Systems (often also referred to as "processes") enable your group to transform information, materials, and knowledge into value in the form of commercially viable products or services, new knowledge or ideas, productive relationships, or anything else the larger organization considers essential. Again, as with structure, ask yourself whether the processes currently in place support the strategy. That is, will those processes enable your group to meet—or even exceed—the goals laid out in the strategy?

Keep in mind that the extent and types of processes you need depend on whether your primary goal is to drive flawless execution or stimulate innovation.[4] You can't hope to achieve high levels of quality and reliability (and low costs) without an intensive focus on developing processes that specify both the ends and the means (methods, techniques, tools) in exquisite detail. Obvious examples of this are manufacturing plants and service delivery organizations. But these same sorts of processes can impede innovation. So if stimulating innovation is your goal, you need to develop processes that focus more on defining ends and rigorously checking progress toward achieving them at key milestones, and not so much on controlling means.

### Doing Process Analysis

A credit card company that sought to identify its fundamental processes came up with the results shown in table 6-1. They then mapped and improved each of these processes, developing appropriate measurement schemes and altering reward systems to better align behaviors. They also focused on identifying key bottlenecks. For critical tasks that were insufficiently under control, they revamped procedures and introduced new support tools. The result was a dramatic increase in both customer satisfaction and the productivity of the organization.

Your unit or group may have just as many processes as the credit card company. Your first challenge is to identify those processes, and then to decide which of them are most important to your strategy. Those vital activities are your *core processes*. For example, suppose your group's strategy emphasizes cus-

**TABLE 6-1**

## Process Analysis Example

| Production/Service-Delivery Processes | Support-Service Processes | Business Processes |
|---|---|---|
| Application processing | Collections | Quality management |
| Credit screening | Customer inquiry | Financial management |
| Credit card production | Relationship management | Human resource management |
| Authorizations management | Information and technology management | |
| Transaction processing | | |
| Billing | | |
| Payment processing | | |

tomer satisfaction over product development. You would want to ensure that all the processes involved in delivery of products or services to customers support that goal.

## Aligning Systems with Structure

If your group's core processes are to support its strategy, they must also align with the unit's *structure* (the way people and work are organized). We can compare this relationship to the human body. Our anatomy—skeleton, musculature, skin, and other components—is the *structural* foundation for the body's normal functions. Our physiology—circulation, respiration, digestion, and so forth—is the set of *systems* that enable the various parts of the body to work together. In organizations as in human bodies, both the structure and the processes must be sound and reinforce one another.

To evaluate the efficiency and effectiveness of each core process, you should examine four aspects:

- **Productivity.** Does the process efficiently transform knowledge, materials, and labor into value?

- **Timeliness.** Does the process deliver the desired value in a timely manner?

- **Reliability.** Is the process sufficiently reliable, or does it break down too often?

- **Quality.** Does the process deliver value in a way that consistently meets required quality standards?

When systems and structure jibe, both elements reinforce each other and the strategy. For example, a customer service organization structured around specific customer segments also shares information across teams and responds effectively to issues that affect all customer groups.

When systems and structure are at odds—such as when different teams compete for the same set of customers, using different sales processes—they hamstring one another and subvert the group's strategy.

### Improving Core Processes

How do you actually improve a core process? Start by making a *process map*—a straightforward diagram of exactly how the tasks in a particular process flow through the individuals and groups who handle them. Figure 6-2 shows a simplified process map for order fulfillment.

Ask the individuals responsible for each stage of the process to chart the process flow from beginning to end. Then ask the team to look for *bottlenecks* and *problem interfaces* between individ-

FIGURE 6 - 2

## A Process Map

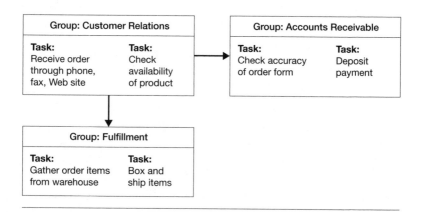

uals responsible for adjacent sets of tasks. For example, errors or delays may occur when someone in customer relations communicates the need for special handling of an order to the fulfillment group. Process failures are commonplace during handoffs of this kind. Work with the team to identify opportunities for high-leverage improvements.

Process analysis stimulates collective learning. It helps the entire group understand exactly who does what, within and between units or groups, to carry out a particular process. Creating a process map also sheds light on how problems arise. You, your boss, and your group can then decide how best to improve the process. You have two options: radical process re-engineering or incremental continual improvement.

A few words of caution. You are probably responsible for a number of processes. If so, manage them as a portfolio. Do not try to introduce radical changes in more than a couple of core processes at a time. Your group will not be able to absorb so much change. As mentioned previously, do not immediately automate problematic processes, a tactic that rarely solves the real problem underlying process inefficiencies. Problems with processes usually center on miscommunication, confused expectations, and misunderstanding about how the business works. Solving deeper problems will yield bigger benefits than simply resorting to automation.

## Developing Your Group's Skills Base

Do your direct reports have the skills and knowledge they need to perform your group's core processes superbly—and thus to support the strategy you have identified? If not, the entire fragile architecture of your group could fall apart. A skills base comprises these four types of knowledge:

- **Individual expertise:** Gained through training, education, and experience

- **Relational knowledge:** An understanding of how to work together to integrate individual knowledge to achieve specified goals

- **Embedded knowledge:** The core technologies on which your group's and performance depend, such as customer databases or R&D technologies

- **Meta-knowledge:** The awareness of where to go to get critical information; for example, through external affiliations such as research institutions and technology partners

### Identifying Gaps and Resources

The overarching goal of assessing your group's capabilities is to identify (1) *critical gaps* between needed and existing skills and knowledge and (2) *underutilized resources* such as partially exploited technologies and squandered expertise. Closing gaps and making better use of underutilized resources can produce enormous gains in performance and productivity.

To identify skills and knowledge gaps, first revisit your strategy and the core processes you identified. Ask yourself what mix of the four types of knowledge is needed to support your group's core processes. Treat this as a visioning exercise in which you imagine the ideal knowledge mix. Then assess your group's existing skills, knowledge, and technologies. What gaps do you see? Which of them can be repaired quickly and which will take more time?

To identify underutilized resources, search for individuals or groups in your unit who have performed much better than

average. What has enabled them to do so? Do they enjoy resources (technologies, methods, materials, and support from
key people) that could be exported to the rest of your unit?
Have promising product ideas been sitting on the shelf because
of lack of interest or investment? Could existing production
resources be adapted to serve new sets of customers?

## Understanding Your Group's Culture

Culture surrounds and influences the other four elements of
organizational architecture, shaping thinking about strategy,
structure, systems, and skills. Indeed, the most important business problems you will face in your new situation will likely all
have a cultural dimension.

Your organization's culture consists of the norms and values
that shape team members' behavior, attitudes, and expectations. An organization's culture cues its people about what to
do and not do. Often, as discussed previously, there are fundamental assumptions about how things work that are so embedded and long-standing that people are not even aware of their
existence.

Cultural habits and norms have an especially frustrating way
of reinforcing the status quo—no matter how much the status
quo needs changing! So, it is vital that you diagnose problems
in your group's existing culture and address them early. Only
then can the culture fully support the group's strategy and align
smoothly with the other pieces of the group's architecture—
structure, systems, and skills.

To understand your group's culture, you must peer below
the surface-level signals of group culture, such as logos, styles of
dress, and ways of communicating or interacting, as well as the
social norms, or shared rules that guide behavior. Search for

the deepest assumptions group members take for granted. For a new leader who is trying to align the various dimensions of his or her group behind the identified strategy, the most relevant assumptions involve the following:

- **Power.** Who do employees think can legitimately exercise authority and make decisions?

- **Value.** What actions and outcomes do employees believe create value? Value can take such forms as making profits, satisfying customers, promoting innovation, creating supportive working environments, and so forth.

How do you tease out fundamental assumptions? To understand assumptions about power, look at how decisions were made in the past. For example, who deferred to whom? To understand assumptions about value, look at how people spend their time and what energizes them most. For instance, do team members seem to focus most on forging positive, collaborative relationships with one another? Do they make customer service a priority? Do they spend most of their time trying to generate promising new product ideas? Is precision in execution valued?

### Initiating Cultural Change

You can't hope to do more than diagnose the culture and begin to work on changing some behaviors in the first 90 days. The following list sets forth five ways to begin cultural change. Whichever methods you use, aim for cultural changes that will align with your group's strategy, structure, systems, and skills.

- **Change performance measures and incentives.** Change the metrics by which you judge success. Then align employees' objectives with those new measures. For instance, consider changing the balance between individual and group incentives. Does success require people to work closely and coordinate with one another—for example, in a new-product development team? If so, then put more weight on group incentives. Do people in your group operate independently—for example, in a sales unit? If so, and if their individual contributions to the business can be measured, then place more emphasis on individual incentives.

- **Set up pilot projects.** Give employees opportunities to experiment with new tools and behaviors. For example, set up a task force to experiment with an innovative approach to production or to tackle problems with distribution.

- **Bring in new people.** Judiciously bring in people from the outside to stimulate creative thinking and discipline among group members. A new person could be a substance expert in a key area—for example, new-product development or R&D management. Alternatively, you could bring in a process consultant—someone with a strong business background, but who focuses on running the process of group dialogue and supports your efforts to implement change.

- **Promote collective learning.** Expose group members to new ways of operating and thinking about the business—for instance, new perspectives on customers and competitors. One idea is to engage in some benchmarking of best-in-class organizations.

- **Engage in collective visioning.** Find ways to bring people together in creative ways specifically to envision new approaches to doing things. For example, schedule an off-site meeting to brainstorm ideas for improving existing processes.

## Getting Aligned

Draw on all this analysis to develop a plan for aligning your organization. If you are repeatedly frustrated in your efforts to get people to adopt more productive behaviors, step back and ask whether organizational misalignments might be creating problems.

### ACCELERATION CHECKLIST

1. What are your provisional observations about misalignments among strategy, structure, systems, skills, and culture? How will you dig deeper to confirm or refine your impressions?

2. What decisions about customers, capital, capabilities, and commitments do you need to make? How and when will you make these decisions?

3. What is your current assessment of the coherence of the organization's strategy? Of its adequacy? What are your current thoughts about changing your organization's strategy?

4. What are the strengths and weaknesses of the organization's structure? What are you thinking about potential structural changes?

5. What are the core processes in your organization?
   How well are they performing? What are your priorities for process improvement?

6. What skills gaps and underutilized resources have you identified? What are your priorities for strengthening the skills base?

7. What are the functional and dysfunctional elements of the culture? What can you begin to do to change the culture?

# 7

# Build Your Team

W HEN LIAM GEFFEN was appointed to lead a troubled unit of an instrumentation company, he knew he was in for an uphill climb. The extent of the challenge became clearer when he read the previous year's performance evaluations for his new team. Everyone was either outstanding or marginal; there was nobody in between. Clearly, his predecessor had played favorites.

Conversations with his new direct reports confirmed Liam's suspicion that the performance evaluations were skewed. In particular, the head of marketing seemed reasonably competent but by no means a minor god. Unfortunately, he believed his own press. The head of sales struck Liam as a solid performer who had been blamed for poor judgment calls by Liam's predecessor. The relationship between marketing and sales was understandably tense.

Liam recognized that one or both would probably have to go. He met with them separately and bluntly told them how he viewed their performance ratings. He then laid out detailed two-month plans for each. Meanwhile he and his VP for human resources quietly launched a search for a new head of marketing. Liam also held skip-level meetings with midlevel people in sales, both to assess the depth of talent and to look for promising candidates for the top job.

By the end of his third month, Liam had signaled the head of marketing that he would not make it; he soon left. Meanwhile, the head of sales had risen to Liam's challenge. Liam gave her more opportunities, eliciting even better performance. Eventually Liam had enough confidence in her to give her overall responsibility for sales and marketing.

Liam Geffen recognized that he couldn't afford to have the wrong people on his team. If, like him, you inherit a group of direct reports, it is essential to *build your team* to marshal the talent you need to achieve superior results. The most important decisions you make in your first 90 days will probably be about the people on your team. If you succeed in creating a high-performance team, you can exert tremendous leverage in value creation. If not, you will face severe difficulties, for no leader can hope to achieve much alone. Bad early personnel choices will almost certainly haunt you. As one experienced manager put it, "Hire in haste, repent at leisure."

Finding the right people is essential, but it is not enough. Begin by assessing existing team members to decide who will stay and who will have to go. Then devise a plan for getting new people and moving the people you retain into the right positions—without doing too much damage to short-term performance in the process. Even this is not enough: You still need to put in place goals, incentives, and performance measures that will propel your team in the desired directions. Finally, you must establish new processes to promote teamwork. This chapter will walk you through these steps.

## Avoiding Common Traps

Many new leaders stumble when it comes to building a winning team. The result may be a significant delay in reaching the breakeven point, or it may be outright derailment. These are some of the characteristic traps into which they fall:

- **Keeping the existing team too long.** Some leaders clean house too precipitously, but it is more common to keep people longer than is wise. Whether because of hubris ("These people have not performed well because they lacked a leader like me") or because they shy away from tough personnel calls, leaders end up with less-than-outstanding teams. This means they will either have to shoulder more of the load themselves or fall short of their goals. One experienced executive put it this way: "You always feel you can fix anything. But you can't. And you can't let [personnel issues] fester. If [some people on the team] are not performing, their peers know it and your peers know it." A good rule of thumb is that you should decide by the end of your first 90 days who will remain and who will go. By the end of six months, you should have communicated your planned personnel changes to key stakeholders, especially your boss and HR. If you wait much longer, the team becomes "yours" and change becomes increasingly difficult to justify and carry out. Naturally, the time frame depends on the $ST_ARS$ situation you are confronting: It may be shorter in a turnaround and longer in a sustaining-success situation. The key is to establish some deadlines for reaching conclusions

about your team and taking action within your 90-day
plan, and then to stick to them.

- **Not repairing the airplane.** Unless you are in a start-up,
  you do not get to build a team from scratch: You
  inherit a team and have to mold it into what you need
  to achieve your A-item priorities. The process of mold-
  ing a team is like repairing an airplane in midflight.
  You will not reach your destination if you ignore the
  necessary repairs. But you do not want to crash the airplane while trying to fix it. This situation can present a
  dilemma: It is essential to replace people, but some of
  them are essential to help run the business in the short
  run. What do you do? You develop options as quickly as
  you can. This may mean hiring people into temporary
  positions so they learn the ropes, or exploring whether
  people further down in the organization can meet the
  challenge.

- **Not working organizational alignment and team restructuring issues in parallel.** A ship's captain cannot make
  the right choices about his crew without knowing the
  destination, the route, and the ship. Likewise, you can't
  build your team before reaching clarity about changes
  in strategy, structure, systems, and skills. Otherwise, you
  could end up with the right people in the wrong jobs.
  As figure 7-1 illustrates, your efforts to assess the organization and achieve alignment should go on in parallel
  with assessment of the team and necessary personnel
  changes.

- **Not holding onto the good people.** One experienced
  manager shared some hard-won lessons about the

FIGURE 7-1

## Synchronizing Architectural Alignment and Team Restructuring

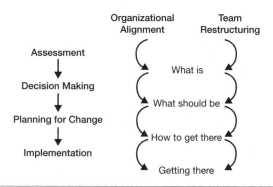

dangers of losing good people. "When you shake the tree," she said, "good people can fall out too." Her point is that uncertainty about who will and will not be on the team can lead your best people to make moves elsewhere. Although there are real constraints on what you can say about who will stay and who will go, you should look for ways to signal to the top performers that you recognize their capabilities. A little reassurance goes a long way.

- **Undertaking team building before the core team is in place.** It is tempting to launch team-building activities, such as joint problem solving, brainstorming, and visioning, right away. New leaders with a consensus-building style often are eager to tap the insights of their direct reports. But this approach poses a danger: It strengthens bonds in a group, some of whose members may be leaving. So avoid explicit team-building activities until the team you want is in place. This does not mean, of course, that you should avoid meeting as a group.

- **Making implementation-dependent decisions too early.`** When successful implementation requires buy-in from your team, you should judiciously defer making decisions until its core members are in place. There will be decisions you cannot afford to delay. But it can be especially difficult to implement decisions that commit new people to courses of action they had no part in defining. So carefully weigh the benefits of moving quickly on major initiatives against the lost opportunity of gaining buy-in from the people you will bring on board later.

- **Trying to do it all yourself.**  Finally, keep in mind that the process of restructuring a team is fraught with emotional, legal, and company policy complications. Do *not* try to undertake this on your own. Find out who can best advise you and help you chart a strategy. The support of a good HR person is indispensable to any effort to restructure a team.

## Assessing Your Existing Team

You are likely to inherit some good performers, some average ones, and some who are simply not up to the job. You will also inherit a group with its own internal dynamics and politics—some members may even have hoped for your job. During your first 30 to 60 days, you need to sort out who's who, what roles each individual plays, and how the group has worked in the past.

### Establish Your Criteria

You will inevitably find yourself forming impressions of team members as you meet them. Don't suppress these early reactions, but step back from them and undertake a more rigorous evaluation.

The starting point is to be self-conscious about the *criteria* you will explicitly or implicitly use to evaluate people who report to you. Consider these six criteria:

- **Competence.** Does this person have the technical competence and experience to do the job effectively?

- **Judgment.** Does this person exercise good judgment, especially under pressure or when faced with making sacrifices for the greater good?

- **Energy.** Does this team member bring the right kind of energy to the job, or is he or she burned out or disengaged?

- **Focus.** Is this person capable of setting priorities and sticking to them, or prone to "riding off in all directions"?

- **Relationships.** Does this individual get along with others on the team and support collective decision making, or is he or she difficult to work with?

- **Trust.** Can you trust this person to keep his or her word and follow through on commitments?

To get a quick read on the criteria you use, fill out table 7-1. Allow yourself 100 points to divide among the six criteria according to the *relative weight* you place on them when you

**TABLE 7 - 1**

## Assessment of Evaluative Criteria

| Evaluative Criteria | Relative Weights (Divide 100 points among the six issues) | Threshold Issue (Designate with an asterisk) |
|---|---|---|
| Competence | | |
| Judgment | | |
| Energy | | |
| Focus | | |
| Relationships | | |
| Trust | | |

evaluate direct reports. Record those numbers in the middle column, making sure that they add up to 100. Now identify one of these criteria as your "threshold issue," meaning that if a person does not meet a basic threshold on that dimension, nothing else matters. Label your threshold issue with an asterisk in the right-hand column.

Now step back. Does this accurately represent the values you apply when you evaluate direct reports? If so, does this analysis suggest any potential blind spots in the way you evaluate people?

Your assessments are likely to reflect certain assumptions about what you can and can't change in the people who work for you. If you score relationships low and judgment high, for example, you may think that relationships within your team are something you can influence, whereas you cannot influence judgment. Likewise, you may have designated trust as a threshold issue—many leaders do—because you believe that you must be able to trust those who work for you and because you think trustworthiness is a trait that cannot be changed.

### Factor in the Situation

To what extent should your evaluative criteria vary depending on the situation you are facing? Potentially a lot. Suppose, for example, that you are taking a new job as vice president of sales, managing a geographically scattered group of regional sales managers. How would your criteria for evaluating people differ from those you would apply if you had been named to lead a new-product development project?

These jobs differ sharply in the extent to which your direct reports (1) operate independently and (2) are dispersed geographically. If your direct reports operate more or less independently, their capacity to work together will be far less important than if you were managing an interdependent product development team. On the other hand, the fact that your people are geographically dispersed may restrict your ability to develop them. If so, you will want them to have threshold levels of competence and judgment.

The criteria you apply may also depend on whether you are in a start-up, turnaround, realignment, or sustaining-success situation. In a sustaining-success situation, for example, you may have the time to develop one or two high-potential members of your team. In a turnaround, by contrast, you need people who can perform at a high level right away. Likewise, in a start-up you may be willing to trade off some trust for a higher level of energy and focus, whereas this would not be the case in a sustaining-success situation.

It is worthwhile to spend some time thinking about the criteria you will use to evaluate your new team. Having done so, you will be better prepared to make a rigorous and systematic evaluation.

## Assess Your People

When you begin to assess each team member using the criteria you have developed, the first test is whether any of them fail to meet your threshold requirements. If so, begin planning to replace them. But merely surviving the basic hurdle does not mean they are keepers. Go on to the next step: Evaluate their strengths and weaknesses, factoring in the relative value you assign to each criterion. Now who makes the grade and who does not?

Meet one-on-one with each member of your new team as soon as possible. Depending on your style, these early meetings might take the form of informal discussions, formal reviews, or a combination, but your own preparation and focus should be standardized:

1. **Prepare for each meeting.**  Review available personnel history, performance data, and other appraisals. Familiarize yourself with each person's technical or professional skills so you can assess how he or she functions on the team.

2. **Ask probing questions.**  As we saw in chapter 2 on learning, ask each person the *same* set of questions, for example:

   • What do you think of our existing strategy?

   • What are the biggest challenges and opportunities facing us in the short term? In the long term?

- What resources could we leverage more effectively?

- How could we improve the way the team works together?

- If you were in my position, what would you *most* want to pay attention to?

3. **Look for verbal and nonverbal clues.** Note choices of words, body language, and hot buttons.

- Notice what the individual does not say. Does the person volunteer information or do you have to extract it? Does the person take responsibility for problems in his or her area? Make excuses? Blame others?

- How consistent are the individual's facial expressions and body language with his or her words?

- What topics elicit strong emotional responses? These hot buttons provide clues to what motivates the individual and what kinds of changes he or she would by energized by.

- Outside of these one-on-one meetings, notice how the individual relates to other team members. Do relations with other team members appear cordial and productive? Tense and competitive? Judgmental or reserved?

### Test Their Judgment

Make sure you are assessing *judgment* and not technical competence or raw intelligence. Some very bright people have lousy judgment, and some people of average competence have extraordinary judgment. It is essential to be clear about the mix of knowledge and judgment you need from key people.

168 The First 90 Days

One way to assess judgment is to work with a person for an extended time and observe whether he or she is able to (1) make sound predictions and (2) develop good strategies for avoiding problems. Both abilities draw on an individual's *mental models,* or ways of identifying the essential features and dynamics of emerging situations and translating those insights into effective action. This is what expert judgment is all about. The problem, of course, is that you don't have much time, and it can take a while to find out whether someone did or did not make good predictions. Fortunately, there are ways you can accelerate this process.

One way is to test people's judgment in a domain in which feedback on their prediction abilities will emerge relatively quickly. Experiment with the following approach. Ask individuals whose judgment you want to evaluate about a topic that they are passionate about outside work. It could be politics or cooking or baseball; it doesn't matter. Challenge them to make predictions: "Who do you think is going to do better in the debate?" "What does it take to bake a perfect soufflé?" "Which team will win the game tonight?" Press them to commit themselves—unwillingness to go out on a limb is a warning sign in itself. Then probe why they think their predictions are correct. Does the rationale make sense? If possible, follow up to see what happens.

What you are testing is a person's capacity to *exercise expert judgment* in a particular domain. Someone who has become an expert in a private domain is likely to have done so in his or her chosen field of business too, given enough passion about it. However you do it, the key is to find ways, beyond just waiting to see how people perform on the job, to probe for the hallmarks of expertise.

## Evaluate Key Functional People

If you are managing a team whose members have diverse functional expertise—such as marketing, finance, operations, and R&D—you will need to get a handle on their competence in their respective areas. This can be daunting, especially for first-time general managers. If you are an insider, try to solicit the opinions of people you respect and trust in each function who know the individuals on your team.

If you are entering a general-management role, consider developing your own evaluation template for each of the key functions. A good template consists of guidelines and warning signs for evaluating people in functions such as marketing, sales, finance, and operations. To develop each template, talk to experienced managers about what they look for in these functions.

## Assess the Team as a Whole

Besides evaluating individual team members, assess how the entire group works. Use these techniques for spotting problems in the team's overall dynamics:

- **Study the data.** Read reports and team meeting minutes. If your organization conducts climate or morale surveys of individual units, examine these as well.

- **Systematically ask questions.** Assess the individual responses to the common set of questions you asked when you met with individual team members. Are their answers overly consistent? If so, this may suggest an agreed-on party line, but it could also mean that everyone genuinely shares the same impressions of what's going on. It will be up to you to evaluate what you observe. Do the responses show little consistency? If so, the team may lack coherence.

- **Probe group dynamics.** Observe how the team interacts in your early meetings. Do you detect any alliances? Particular attitudes? Leadership roles? Who defers to whom on a given topic? When one person is speaking, do others roll their eyes or otherwise express disagreement or frustration? Pay attention to these signs to test your early insights and detect coalitions and conflicts.

## Restructuring Your Team

By now, your evaluation of individual team members' capabilities should have equipped you to figure out how best to deal with each person. Using the insights you have gained, assign each team member to one of the following categories:

- **Keep in place.** The person is performing well in his or her current job.

- **Keep and develop.** The individual needs development, when time allows.

- **Move to another position.** The person is a strong performer but is not in a position that makes the most of his or her skills or personal qualities.

- **Observe for a while.** The individual requires watching and needs a personal development plan.

- **Replace (low priority).** The person should be replaced, but the situation is not urgent.

- **Replace (high priority).** The person should be replaced as soon as possible.

## Consider Alternatives to Outright Termination

You may be tempted to begin right away letting go the people you have decided to replace. But take a moment first to consider alternatives. Letting an employee go can be difficult and time-consuming. Even if poor performance is well documented, the termination process can take months or longer. If there is no paper trail regarding poor performance, it will take time to document.

Fortunately, you do have some alternatives. Often, a poor performer will decide to move on of his or her own accord in response to a clear message from you. Alternatively, you can work with human resources to shift the person to a more suitable position:

- **Move them laterally.** Shift the person to a position on the team that better suits his or her skills. This is unlikely to be a permanent solution for a problem performer, but it can help you work through the short-term problem of keeping the organization running while you look for the right person to fill the slot.

- **Move the person elsewhere in the organization.** Work with human resources to help the person find a suitable position in the larger organization. Sometimes, if handled well, this move can benefit you, the individual, and the organization overall. But don't pursue this solution unless you are genuinely convinced the person can perform well in the new situation. Simply shifting a problem performer onto someone else's shoulders will damage your reputation.

### Develop Backups

To keep your team functioning while you build the best possible long-term configuration, you may need to keep an under-
performer on the job while searching for a replacement. As
soon as you are reasonably sure that someone is not going to
make it, begin looking discreetly for a successor. Evaluate other
people on your team and elsewhere in the organization for
the potential to move up. Use skip-level meetings and regular
reporting sessions to evaluate the talent pool. Ask human resources to launch a search.

### Treat People Respectfully

During every phase of the team-restructuring process, take
pains to treat *everyone* with respect. Even if people in your unit
agree that a particular person should be replaced, your reputation will suffer if they view your actions as unfair. Do what you
can to show people the care with which you are assessing team
members' capabilities and the fit between jobs and individuals.
Your direct reports will form lasting impressions of you based
on how you manage this part of your job.

## Aligning Goals, Incentives, and Measures

Having the right people on the team is essential, but it's not
enough. To achieve your A-item priorities and secure early
wins, you will need to define how each team member can best
support those key goals. This process calls for breaking down
large goals into their component pieces and working with your
team to assign responsibility for each element to a particular

team member. Then it calls for making each individual accountable for managing his or her goals. How do you encourage accountability? The short answer is: through effective incentives and clear criteria for measuring performance.

## Designing Incentive Systems

A blend of push and pull tools works best to motivate a team and shape behavior (see figure 7-2). *Push tools,* such as compensation plans, performance measurement systems, annual budgets, and the like, motivate people through authority, loyalty, fear, and expectation of reward for productive work. *Pull tools,* such as a compelling vision, inspire people by invoking a positive and exciting image of the future.

The particular mix of tools you use will depend on your assessment of how people on your team prefer to be motivated. Your high-energy go-getters will probably respond most enthusiastically to pull incentives. With more methodical and risk-averse folks, push tools may prove more effective.

How do you go about combining these two types of incentives? You have several options. A baseline question to ask

FIGURE 7 - 2

### Using Push and Pull Tools to Motivate People

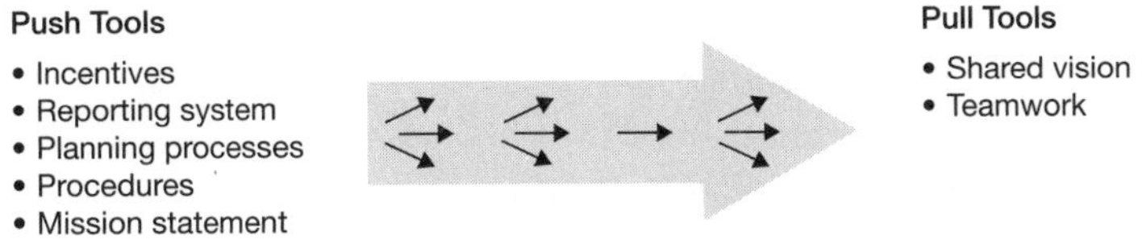

Push Tools
- Incentives
- Reporting system
- Planning processes
- Procedures
- Mission statement

Pull Tools
- Shared vision
- Teamwork

yourself is how you will want to reward team members for achieving goals. What mix of *monetary* and *nonmonetary* rewards will you employ?

It is equally important to decide whether to base rewards on *individual* or *collective* performance. Do you need a high-performing *team*, or is a high-performing *group* enough? The distinction is an important one. If your direct reports work essentially independently, and the group's success hinges chiefly on individual achievement, you don't need to promote teamwork and should consider an individual incentive system. If success depends largely on cooperation among your direct reports and integration of their expertise, true teamwork is essential and you should use group goals and incentives to gain alignment.

Usually, you will want to create incentives for both individual excellence (when your direct reports undertake independent tasks) and for team excellence (when they undertake interdependent tasks). The correct mix of individual and group rewards depends on the relative importance of independent and interdependent activity for the overall success of your unit. (See "The Incentive Equation.")

Designing incentive systems is a challenge, but the dangers of incentive misalignment are great. You need your direct reports to act as agents for you, whether they are undertaking individual responsibilities or collective ones. You don't want to give them incentives to pursue individual goals when true teamwork is necessary, or vice versa.

### Defining Performance Metrics

Establishing—and sticking to—clear and explicit performance metrics is the best way to encourage accountability. That

## The Incentive Equation

The *incentive equation* defines the mix of incentives that you will use to motivate desired performance. Here are the basic formulas:

A.    Total reward = non-monetary reward + monetary reward

The relative sizes of nonmonetary and monetary reward depend on (1) the availability of nonmonetary rewards such as advancement and recognition, and (2) their perceived importance to the people involved.

B.            Monetary Reward = fixed compensation
                    + performance-based compensation

The relative sizes of fixed and performance-based compensation depend on (1) the extent of observability and measurability of peoples' contributions, and (2) the time lag between performance and results. The lower the observability or measurability of contributions and longer the time lag, the more you should rely on fixed compensation.

C.   Performance-based compensation = individual performance-
      based compensation + group performance-based compensation

The relative sizes of individual and group-based performance compensation depend on the extent of interdependence of contributions. If superior performance comes from the sum of independent efforts, then individual performance should be rewarded (for example, in a sales group). If group cooperation and integration is critical, then group-based incentives should get more weight (for example, in a new-product development team). Note that there may be several levels of group-based incentives—team, unit, and company as a whole.

is, select performance measures that will let you know unambiguously whether a team member has achieved his or her goals.

Avoid ambiguously defined goals, such as "Improve sales" or "Decrease product development time." Instead, define goals in terms that can be quantified. For instance, "Increase sales of product X by 15 to 30 percent over the fourth quarter of this year," or "Decrease development time on product line Y from 12 months to six months within the next two years."

## Establishing New Team Processes

Once the team and their goals and incentives have been established, the next step is to think through how you want the team to work. That is, what processes will shape how the team gets its collective job done? Teams vary strikingly in how they handle meetings, make decisions, resolve conflict, and divide responsibilities and tasks. You will probably want to introduce new ways of doing things. But take care not to plunge into this task precipitously. First, familiarize yourself thoroughly with how your team worked before your arrival, and how effective its processes were. That way, you can preserve what worked well and change what did not.

### Assess Your Team's Existing Processes

How can you get a handle on your team's existing processes quickly? Talk to team members and support staff, and to your new boss or your predecessor. Get them to brief you on their functions and walk you through the key processes. Read meeting minutes and team reports. Probe for answers to the following questions:

- **Participants' roles.** Who influenced your predecessor most? Who played devil's advocate? Who was the innovator? Who avoided uncertainty? To whom did everyone else listen most attentively? Who was the peacemaker? The rabble-rouser?

- **Team meetings.** How often did your team meet? Who participated? Who set the agendas for meetings?

- **Decision making.** Who made what kinds of decisions? Who was consulted on decisions? Who was told once decisions were made?

- **Leadership style.** What leadership style did your predecessor prefer? That is, how did he or she prefer to learn, communicate, motivate, and handle decisions? How does your predecessor's leadership style compare with yours? If your styles differ markedly, how will you address the likely impact of those differences on your team?

### Target Processes for Change

Once you grasp how your team functioned in the past—and what did and did not work well—it is time to use what you have learned and establish the new processes you judge necessary. Many leaders decide, for example, that their team's meeting and decision-making processes would benefit from revision. If this is true of you, begin spelling out in specific terms what changes you envision. How often will the team meet? Who will attend which meetings? How will agendas be established and circulated? Setting up clear and effective processes will help your team coalesce and secure some early wins as a group.

## Altering Who Participates

One common team process problem—and a great opportunity to send a message that change is coming—concerns who participates in core team meetings. In some organizations, key meetings are too inclusive, with too many people participating in discussions and decision making. If this is the case, then move rapidly to reduce the size of the core group and streamline the meetings, sending the message that you value efficiency and focus. In other organizations, key meetings are too exclusive, with people with potentially important opinions and information being systematically excluded. If this is the case, then rapidly move to judiciously broaden participation, sending the message that you will not be playing favorites or listening to just a few points of view.

## Managing Decision Making

Decision making is another fertile area for potential improvement. Few team leaders do a good job of managing decision making. In part, this is because different types of decisions call for different decision-making processes; most team leaders stick with one approach. They do this because they have a style with which they are comfortable and because they believe they need to be consistent or risk confusing their direct reports.

Research I've done in collaboration with my colleagues Amy Edmondson and Mike Roberto suggests that this is wrong-headed.[1] The key is to have a framework for understanding and communicating why different decisions will be approached in different ways.

Think of the different ways that teams can make decisions. As pictured in figure 7-3, possible approaches can be arrayed on a

FIGURE 7 - 3

## Group Decision-Making Spectrum

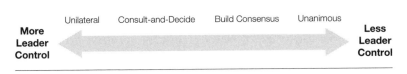

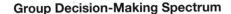

spectrum ranging from unilateral decision making at one end to unanimous consent at the other. In unilateral decision making, the leader simply makes the call, either without consultation or with limited consultation with personal advisers. The risks associated with this approach are obvious: You may miss critical information and insights and get only lukewarm support for implementation.

At the other extreme, processes that require unanimous consent from more than a few people tend to suffer from *decision diffusion*. They go on and on, never reaching closure. Or, if a decision does get made, it is often a lowest-common-denominator compromise. In either case, critical opportunities and threats are not addressed effectively.

Between these two extremes are the decision-making processes that most leaders use: *consult-and-decide* and *build consensus*. When a leader solicits information and advice from direct reports—individually or as a group, or both—but reserves the right to make the final call, he or she is using a consult-and-decide approach. In effect he or she separates the "information gathering and analysis" process from the "evaluating and reaching closure" process, harnessing the group for one but not the other.

In the build-consensus process, the leader both seeks information and analysis and seeks buy-in from the group for any decision. The goal is not full consensus but sufficient consensus. This means that a critical mass of the group believes the decision to be the right one and, critically, that the rest agree that they can live with and support implementation of the decision.

When should you choose one process over the other? The answer is emphatically *not* "If I am under time pressure, I will use consult-and-decide." Why? Because although it may be true that you reach a *decision* quicker by the consult-and-decide route, you won't necessarily reach the *desired outcome* faster. In fact, you may end up consuming a lot of time trying to sell the decision after the fact, or finding out that people are not energetically implementing it and having to pressure them. Those who suffer from the action imperative are most at risk of this; they want to "reach closure" by making the call, but may jeopardize their end goals in the process.

The following rules of thumb can help you figure out which decision-making process to use:

- If the decision is likely to be highly divisive—creating winners and losers—then you usually are better off using consult-and-decide and taking the heat. A build-consensus process will both fail to reach a good outcome and get everyone mad at one another in the process. Put another way, decisions about sharing losses or pain among a group of people are best made by the leader.

- If the decision requires energetic support for implementation from people whose performance you cannot adequately observe and control, then you usually are better off using a build-consensus process. You may get to a decision more quickly using consult-and-decide, but not to the desired outcome.

- If you are managing a team of people who are relatively inexperienced, then you usually are better off relying more on consult-and-decide until you have taken the measure of the team and developed their capabilities. If you try to adopt a build-consensus approach with an inexperienced team, you risk getting frustrated and imposing a decision anyway, which effectively undercuts teamwork.

- If you are put in charge of a group of people with whom you need to establish your authority (such as supervising former peers), then you are better off relying on consult-and-decide to make some key early decisions. You can relax and rely more on building consensus once people see that you have the steadiness and insight to make tough calls.

Your approach to decision making will also vary depending on which of the ST$_A$RS situations you are in. Start-ups and turn-arounds are situations in which consult-and-decide often works well. The problems tend to be technical (markets, products, technologies) rather than cultural and political in nature. Also, people may be hungry for "strong" leadership, which often is associated with a consult-and-decide style. To be effective in realignment and sustaining-success situations, by contrast, leaders often need to deal with strong intact teams and to confront cultural and political issues. These sorts of issues are typically best addressed with the build-consensus approach.

To alter your approach to decision making depending on the nature of the decision to be made, you will sometimes have to restrain your natural inclinations. You are likely to have a preference for either consult-and-decide or build-consensus decision making. But preferences are not destiny. If you are a consult-and-decide person, you should consider experimenting with building (sufficient) consensus in suitable situations. If you are a build-consensus person, you should feel free to adopt a consult-and-decide approach when it is appropriate to do so.

To avoid confusion, consider explaining to your direct reports what process you are going to use and why. More important, strive to run a *fair process*.[2] Even if people do not agree with the final decision, they often will support it if they feel (1) that their views and interests have been heard and taken seriously and (2) that you have given them a plausible rationale for why you made the call you did. The corollary is: Don't engage in a charade of consensus building—an effort to build support for a decision already made. This rarely fools anyone, creates cynicism, and undercuts implementation. You are better off to simply use consult-and-decide.

Finally, you often can shift between build-consensus and consult-and-decide modes as you gain deeper insight into peoples' interests and positions. It may make sense, for example, to begin in a consensus-building mode but reserve the right to shift to consult-and-decide if the process is becoming too divisive. It also may make sense to begin with consult-and-decide and shift to build-consensus if it emerges that energetic implementation is critical and consensus is possible.

## Jump-Starting the Team

You will know you have been successful in building your team when you reach the breakeven point—when the energy the team creates is greater than the energy you need to put into it. It will take a while before that happens; you have to charge the battery before you can start the engine.

## ACCELERATION CHECKLIST

1. What are your criteria for assessing the performance of members of your team? How do the people you inherited stack up against these criteria?

2. What personnel changes do you need to make? Which changes are urgent and which can wait? How will you create backups and options?

3. What process will you put in place to make the high-priority changes? What can you do to preserve the dignity of the people affected?

4. What help will you need with the restructuring process, and where are you going to find it?

5. Do you need to amend existing incentives and measures? Do people in your unit have incentives to cooperate and compete in productive ways?

6. How do you want your new team to operate? What roles do you want people to play? Do you need to shrink the core team or expand it?

7. How do you plan to manage decision making? Will you start off emphasizing a consult-and-decide or a build-consensus approach?

# 8

# Create Coalitions

AFTER FIVE YEARS as a country manager at a medical devices company, Jack Daley was put in charge of global marketing for a key product line in the orthopedics operating division. Operating divisions developed new products and "sold" them internally to the various country-based sales and marketing groups.

Over the years, Jack had become accustomed to wielding authority to get things done. Country managers had P&L responsibility and decided which products their sales reps would push. Often compared to feudal lords, country managers had considerable control over their own activities and enjoyed high status in the business communities of their respective countries. Predictably, country managers were prone to arrogance and renowned for dressing down those who presumed to know how to sell in local markets.

Suddenly Jack was on the other side of the table: To succeed, he had to persuade his former peers. After some disastrous early meetings in which he tried a hard sell, Jack adjusted his approach. He identified several countries that represented promising potential markets for his product and met with those country managers. He pointed out the benefits of his product and offered to offset the costs of educating sales reps about its features. Then he listened. Several country managers signed on. The product soon won broad acceptance from the other countries—even those who had rejected Jack's earlier approach.

Having found his regular directive approach a bad fit in his new job, Jack Daley saw the need to exert influence without authority. If your success depends on the support of people outside your direct line of command, it is imperative to *create coalitions* to get things done. Direct authority is never enough to win the day. Influence networks—informal bonds among colleagues—can help you marshal backing for your ideas and goals. But it is up to you to build coalitions that will help you achieve your agenda. To do so, you will need an influence strategy. This means figuring out whom you must influence, pinpointing who is likely to support and resist your key initiatives, and persuading "swing voters." Plans for doing this, beginning with the assessment process, should be an integral part of your overall 90-day plan.

## Mapping the Influence Landscape

One common mistake of new leaders is to devote too much of their transition time to the vertical dimension of influence— upward to bosses and downward to direct reports—and not enough to the horizontal dimension, namely, peers and external constituencies. This error is understandable: You naturally gravitate toward the people to whom you report and who report to you. After all, they are the primary channels through whom you will have an impact and leverage yourself.

Sooner or later (probably sooner), though, you will need the support of people over whom you have no direct authority, within the company and externally. You may have little or no relationship capital with these people—no preexisting support and obligations on which to draw. Therefore, you will need to invest thought and energy in building a new base. Start early. It is never a good idea to approach people for the first time when you need something from them; you wouldn't want to introduce yourself to your neighbors in the middle of the night when your house is burning down. Discipline yourself to invest in building relationship capital with people you anticipate needing to work with later.

Think about how you have allocated your time to relationship building so far. Are there people you haven't met yet who are likely to be critical to your success?

### Identify the Key Players

How can you figure out who will be important for your success? To a degree, it will become obvious as you get to know the organization better. But you can accelerate that process. Start by *identifying the key interfaces* between your unit or group and others. Customers and suppliers, within the business and outside, are natural focal points for relationship building.

Another strategy is to *get your boss to connect you.* Request a list of ten key people outside your group whom he or she thinks you should get to know. Then set up early meetings with them. In the spirit of the golden rule of transitions, consider proactively doing the same when you have new direct reports coming on board: Create priority relationship lists for them and help them to make contact.

Another productive approach is to *diagnose informal networks of influence,* or what has been called "the shadow organization" and "the company behind the organization chart."[1] Every organization has such networks, and they usually matter both in making change happen and in blocking change. These networks exist because people tend to defer to others whose opinions they respect on a given set of issues.

As a first step in coalition building, analyze patterns of deference and the sources of power that underlie them. How? Watch carefully in meetings and other interactions to see who defers to whom on crucial issues. Try to trace alliances. Notice to whom people go for advice and insight, and who shares what information and news. Figure out who marshals resources, who is known for taking pains to help friends, and who owes favors to whom.

At the same time, try to identify the sources of power that give particular people influence in the organization. The usual sources of power in an organization are

- Expertise

- Access to information

- Status

- Control of resources, such as budgets and rewards

- Personal loyalty

You can use some of the techniques described in chapter 2 on accelerating learning to gain insight into these political dynamics. Talk to former employees and people who did business with the organization in the past. Seek out the natural historians.

Eventually you will be able to pick out the *opinion leaders:* people who exert disproportionate influence through formal authority, special expertise, or sheer force of personality. If you can convince these vital individuals that your A-item priorities and other goals have merit, broader acceptance of your ideas is likely to follow. By the same token, resistance from them could galvanize broader opposition.

You will also eventually recognize *power coalitions:* groups of people who explicitly or implicitly cooperate to pursue particular goals or protect particular privileges. If these power coalitions support your agenda, you will gain leverage. If they decide to oppose you, you may have no choice but to break them up and build new ones.

### Draw an Influence Map

It can be instructive to summarize what you learn about patterns of influence by drawing an *influence map* like the one illustrated in figure 8-1. It depicts both the flow and the extent of

**FIGURE 8 - 1**

**An Influence Map**

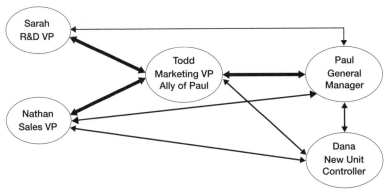

influence among members of a hypothetical business unit. Paul is the general manager of the unit. Todd is the VP of marketing and a long-time ally of Paul's. Nathan and Sarah are VPs of sales and R&D, respectively. Dana, the new unit controller, has created this influence map in an effort to figure out how to advance some key initiatives.

The direction of a given arrow indicates who influences whom. An arrow's width indicates the relative strength with which one individual influences another. Note that influence can flow both ways, depending on the issue. For example, Paul may influence Todd to set certain budgetary goals for marketing. Todd, in turn, may persuade Paul to authorize hiring new personnel.

### Identify Supporters, Opponents, and Convincibles

The point of doing influence mapping is to help you identify supporters, opponents, and "convincibles"—people who can be persuaded with the right influence strategy.

*Supporters* will approve of your agenda because it advances their own interests, because they respect you, or because they see merit in your ideas. To identify your potential supporters, look for the following:

- People who share your vision for the future. If you see a need for thoroughgoing change, look for others who have pushed for changes like those you are promoting.

- People who have been quietly working for change on a small scale, such as a plant engineer who has found an innovative way to significantly reduce waste.

- People new to the company who have not yet become acculturated to its mode of operation.

Whatever supporters' reasons for backing you, do not take their support for granted. It is never enough merely to identify support; you have to solidify and nurture it.

*Opponents* will oppose you no matter what you do. They may believe that you are wrong. Or they may have other reasons for resistance to your agenda, such as the following:

- **Comfort with the status quo.** They resist changes that might undermine their positions or alter established relationships.

- **Fear of looking incompetent.** They fear seeming or feeling incompetent if they have trouble adapting to the changes you are proposing and perform inadequately afterward.

- **Threat to values.** They believe you are promoting a culture that spurns traditional definitions of value or rewards inappropriate behavior.

- **Threat to power.** They fear that the change you are proposing (such as a shift from team-leader decision making to team consensus decision making) would deprive them of power.

- **Negative consequences for key allies.** They fear that your agenda will have negative consequences for others they care about or feel responsible for.

When you meet resistance, try to grasp the reasons behind it before labeling people as implacable opponents. Understanding resisters' motives will equip you to counter the arguments your opponents will marshal. You may find that you can convert some early opponents. For example, you may be able to address fears of incompetence by helping people develop new skills. At the same time, it is essential not to waste valuable time and energy trying to win over staunch opponents.

Finally, *convincibles* are the swing voters: people who are undecided about or indifferent to change, and people you think you could persuade once you understand and appeal to their interests. Once you have identified convincibles, look into what motivates them. People are motivated by different things, such as status, financial security or wealth, job security, positive social and professional relationships with colleagues, and opportunities to tackle new and stimulating challenges. So take the time to try to figure out what *they* perceive their interests to be. Start by putting yourself in their shoes: If you were them, what would you care about? If it is possible to engage them directly in dialogue, then ask questions about how they see the situation, and engage in active listening. If you have connections to other people in their organization, then you should use them to learn. If you don't, you might think about judiciously cultivating them.

Meanwhile, ask yourself whether there are competing forces that might tip convincibles toward resisting you. For example, making them see that their interests are compatible with yours would prompt them to support you, but the threat of losing a comfortable status quo might trigger resistance. Interests and competing forces should be part of what you undertake to learn about the politics of your organization through conversations, exploration of past decisions, and observation of group interactions.

## Using the Tools of Persuasion

Now you are ready to think about persuasion strategies. When I teach groups of new leaders about influence in organizations, I often start with a simple thought experiment. "You are sober, serious professional managers," I say. "But suppose I wanted to get you to do something absurd and embarrassing, such as standing up, bouncing up and down on one foot with your thumbs in your ears singing 'Row, Row, Row Your Boat' at the top of your lungs. How might I persuade you to do that?"

### Shaping Perceptions of Choices

Two influence strategies usually emerge right away: bribery and threats. Both are examples of changing individual incentives to change behavior. Both alter how people perceive their alternatives when they are deciding whether to comply. This is the art of *choice shaping*.

Before bribes are offered or threats uttered, members of the group might perceive their alternatives—status quo and change—as shown in figure 8-2. Status quo means staying in one's seat, while change entails looking silly. Faced with this choice, most people would choose the status quo. People facing change in organizations often see their alternatives in the same way: Should I make uncomfortable changes or stick with the relatively comfortable status quo?

**FIGURE 8 - 2**

**Choice Between Status Quo and Change**

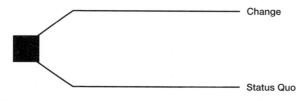

Now suppose I offer people money to do what I ask. The status quo option remains the same, but the attractiveness of the change option increases. Everyone has a price at which he or she would tolerate minor social discomfort because the payoff is sufficiently attractive.

The analogue in organizational change initiatives is: Find ways to *compensate potential losers* to make change more palatable. Of course, there are practical limits on your ability to do this; sometimes the price is simply too high. But it is always worth asking yourself whether you can offer trades or other forms of compensation (such as support for an initiative they care about) to win support.

Now suppose that, instead of offering compensation, I told the group to do as I said or I would get hired goons to break their legs. And suppose that my threat was credible: The doors were locked and the goons were visible, pipes and bars in hand. This influence strategy also alters the group's perceived alternatives. But rather than making the benefits of compliance more attractive, it makes noncompliance more costly. The perceived cost of looking silly remains the same, but the group no longer has the alternative of just sitting tight. The analogue in managing organizational change is: Find ways to *eliminate the status quo as an alternative.* If you can convince people that change is going to happen with or without them, for example, their choice is transformed as shown in figure 8-3.

### Framing Compelling Arguments

Eventually a participant in my demonstration says something like, "All this talk about bribes and threats is distasteful. Why don't you just ask us to do it and see what happens?" The answer is that it is by no means a certainty that people will com-

**FIGURE 8 - 3**

## Choice Between Participating or Having Change Happen Anyway

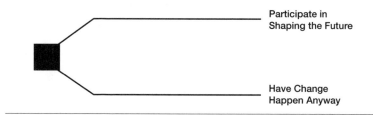

Participate in
Shaping the Future

Have Change
Happen Anyway

ply without a persuasive argument or rationale. So I ask the group, "Suppose I were simply to ask you to do this embarrassing thing. How could I increase the likelihood that you would comply? What rationale could I offer that might either reduce the perceived costs of action or increase the perceived costs of inaction?"

One possible rationale I could offer is that doing what I ask would contribute materially to the educational objectives of the program. If the group believed me and found me credible (because of my expertise and authority as their instructor), my plea might move them. So it can help to marshal persuasive rationales and the data to back them up. A compelling argument for change can function in the same way.

Persuasive appeals can be based on logic and data, or on values and the emotions that values elicit, or on some combination thereof. Reason-based arguments have to directly address the pragmatic interests of the people you want to convince. Value-based arguments aim to trigger emotional reflexes—for example, by evoking patriotism to win support for sacrifices during wartime. Classic values invoked to convince others to embrace potentially painful change are summarized in table 8-1.

TABLE 8 - 1

## Appealing to Core Values

| Core Values | Within the Business Environment |
| --- | --- |
| Loyalty | • Commitment to an ideal<br>• Sacrifice to realize that ideal |
| Commitment and contribution | • Service to customers and suppliers<br>• Creating a better organization, society, or world |
| Individual worth and dignity | • Respect for the individual expressed as elimination of exploitative or patronizing practices and promotion of decency and opportunity for all<br>• Providing the means for individuals to realize their potential |
| Integrity | • Respect for the letter and the spirit of the law<br>• Ethical and honest behavior<br>• Fairness in all interactions |

### Setting Up Action-Forcing Events

How can you get people to take action at all? It is all too easy, even with the best intentions, to defer decisions, delay, and avoid committing scarce resources. When your success requires the coordinated action of many people, delay by a single individual can have a cascade effect, giving others an excuse not to proceed. You must therefore eliminate inaction as an option.

One approach is to set up *action-forcing events*—events that induce people to make commitments or take actions. Those who make commitments should be locked into timetables with incremental implementation milestones. Meetings, review sessions, and deadlines can all sustain momentum: Regular meetings to review progress, and tough questioning of those who fail to reach agreed-on goals, increase the psychological pressure to follow through.

Be careful, though: Avoid pressing for closure until you are confident the balance of forces acting on key people is tipping your way. Otherwise, you could succeed in forcing them to take a stand, but inadvertently push them toward the "opponent" side of the ledger. Again, you need to rely on your conversations with the people involved and with your "intelligence network" to get a sense of where the situation stands.

### Employing Entanglement

Reformulating incentives, framing arguments, and setting up action-forcing events are relatively static persuasion techniques: You figure out how people perceive their choices, and then you craft a mix of push and pull forces that alter those perceptions. Voilà, you get the behavior you want.

But what if moving people from where they are (comfortable with the status quo) to where you want them to be (enthusiastically supporting change) is either impossible to achieve all at once or just too expensive for you? What do you do then?

You could adopt *entanglement strategies* that move people from A to B in a series of small steps rather than a single leap. To return to the example of inducing a group to do something embarrassing, I could start by asking them to stand up. Then I could ask them to stand on one foot, and so on.

One approach is to leverage small commitments into larger ones. If you are trying to launch a new initiative, begin by getting people to agree to participate in an initial organizing meeting. Then get them to commit to a subsequent meeting, then to doing a small piece of analysis, and so on. Entanglement works because each step creates a new psychological reference point for deciding whether to take the next small step. When possible, try to make each step irreversible, like a door that locks

198 The First 90 Days

once it has been passed through. Getting people to make commitments in public, for example, creates a barrier to backsliding, as does getting commitments in writing.

A related technique to overcome resistance to change is a multistage approach to problem solving. Start by getting people to take part in some shared data collection, for example, on how the organization is performing relative to competition. Oversee this process carefully to be sure that they take a hard look at performance using external comparisons. The key at this stage is to get them to recognize that there is a problem or problems that must be dealt with.

When that task is done, shift the focus to gaining a shared definition of the "the problem." What exactly is the problem? Push them hard to engage in root cause analysis, using process analysis tools if helpful. Then get them to work jointly on criteria for evaluating alternative courses of action. What would a "good" solution look like? How should we measure success?

Finally, use the resulting criteria to evaluate the alternatives. How do the various alternative approaches stack up? By the alternative-evaluation stage of this process, many people will accept outcomes they would have rejected at the outset.

Another entanglement strategy is to *use behavior change to drive attitude change.* This may sound backwards, but the attitude/behavior-change equation runs both ways. It is possible to alter people's attitudes (with a compelling argument or evocative vision) and thus to change their behavior. But attitude change, and its close organizational cousin cultural change, is difficult to achieve and to sustain.

It turns out, interestingly enough, that if you can change peoples' *behavior* in desired ways, their *attitudes* will shift to support the new behavior. This occurs because people feel a strong need to preserve consistency between their behavior and their beliefs. The implication for persuasion is clear: It often makes sense to focus first on getting people to act in new ways, such as by changing measurement and incentive systems, rather than trying to change their attitudes. If you get them taking the right actions, the right attitudes will follow.

### Sequencing to Build Momentum

As we have seen, people consistently look to others in their social networks for clues about "right thinking," and defer to others with expertise or status on particular sets of issues. The resulting influence networks can be a formidable barrier to your efforts or a valuable asset, or both.

Let us return once more to the example of asking a group of people to do something embarrassing. Suppose that, in response to my request, a respected member of the group said, "No way I'm doing that. It is disrespectful and foolish." Almost certainly no one else in the group would do what I had asked. But suppose the same person jumped up, grabbed someone else and said, "Let's do it! It'll be fun!" The odds are that everyone else would eventually follow suit. In fact, the last to rise would feel social pressure to do so: "What's the matter with you?"

Now suppose I did an analysis of the group before this exercise and identified the most respected person. Suppose I met with that person before the exercise and enlisted his or her aid as a confederate to make some important points about group dynamics and social influence. The odds are good that this person would agree to do so—and that others would follow.

The fundamental insight is that you can leverage knowledge of influence networks into disproportionate influence on a group with what my colleague Jim Sebenius termed a *sequencing strategy*.[2] The order in which you approach potential allies and convincibles will have a decisive impact on your coalition-building efforts. Why? Once you gain a respected ally, you will typically find it easier to recruit others. As you recruit more allies, your resource base grows. With broader support, the likelihood increases that your agenda will succeed. That optimistic outlook makes it easier to recruit still more supporters.

If you approach the right people first, you can set in motion a *virtuous cycle* (figure 8-4). Therefore, you need to decide carefully who you will approach first, and how you will do it.

Who should you approach first? Focus on the following:

- People with whom you already have supportive relationships

- Individuals whose interests are strongly compatible with yours

**FIGURE 8 - 4**

## The Coalition-Building Cycle

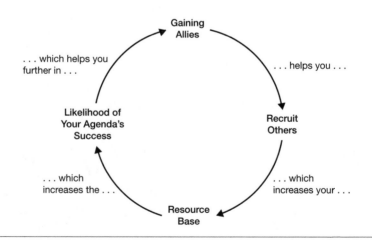

- People who have the critical resources you need to make your agenda succeed

- People with important connections who can recruit more supporters

## Putting It All Together

Coalition building entails consolidating existing sources of support while developing relationships with those whose resources or connections you need to succeed. The sequence in which you consolidate and build support is key. You will also need to persuade convincibles to become supporters rather than opponents.

To consolidate existing support, call on established social and political relationships and strengthen them through regular conversations. Make sure you keep your allies up to date. Pay attention to how they react to changing conditions. You can even provide them with advice for how to counter opponents' arguments. You want to affirm the importance of existing relationships and leverage them into support for your new effort.

### ACCELERATION CHECKLIST

1. Whose support do you most need to succeed? What existing coalitions seem most powerful?

2. What influence networks are most important to you? Who defers to whom on key issues?

3. Who are your potential supporters? Potential opponents? Convincibles? How will you test your hypotheses about support and opposition?

4. What tools of influence will you employ to convince the convincibles? How will you shape potential supporters' perceptions of their interests? Of their options?

5. How can you sequence interactions to build momentum for your initiatives? Are there patterns of deference that you can exploit? Can your supporters help you to recruit other key people?

# 9

# Keep Your Balance

AFTER SIX YEARS in the Manhattan office of a large advertising company, Kipp Erikson was promoted to a senior position at the firm's Canadian unit. He expected the move from New York to Toronto to be a breeze. After all, Canadians and Americans are pretty much alike. Although Canada is officially bilingual, everyone in Toronto spoke English. And the city was safe and reputed to have good restaurants and cultural events.

Kipp moved right away, rented an apartment in downtown Toronto, and dove into the new job with his usual energy. His wife, Irene, an accomplished freelance interior designer, put their co-op apartment up for sale and started preparing their two children, Katherine, 10, and Elizabeth, 7, for a mid-school-year move. Kipp and Irene had talked about postponing moving the children until the end of the school year, four months away, but decided that it was too long to have the family separated.

The first hints of trouble in the new job were subtle. Every time he tried to get something done, Kipp felt like he was wading through molasses. As a lifelong New Yorker accustomed to telling things the way they were, he also found his new colleagues irritatingly polite and conflict averse. (For their part, they were taken aback by a brashness that bordered on insensitivity.) At every opportunity, Kipp complained to Irene that his colleagues refused to engage in hardheaded discussion about the tough issues. And he couldn't find the kind of go-to people he had relied on to get things done in New York.

Four weeks after Kipp started the job, Irene joined him in Toronto to look for a new house and school and to scope out prospects for continuing her freelance design work. Kipp was frustrated with the job and irritable. Irene's unhappiness quickly mounted when she couldn't find a school to her liking. The children had been happily enrolled in an excellent private school. They were displeased about moving and had been making Irene's life miserable. She had calmed them with stories about the adventure of moving to a new country and promises that she would find them a great new school. Dispirited, she told Kipp that she thought they should leave the kids where they were until the end of the year; he agreed.

With Kipp commuting between Toronto and New York, and Irene under pressure as a working single parent, events quickly took a toll on their relationship. Although Irene visited Toronto for a couple of weekends and continued looking into schools, it became clear that her heart was not in the move. Weekends often were stressful, with the children both happy to see Kipp and unhappy about the move. Kipp often arrived back in the office on Mondays tired and unable to concentrate, aggravating his difficulties getting traction and connecting with his colleagues and team. He knew his work performance was suffering, which further increased his stress level.

Eventually he decided to force the issue. Through connections at the company, he found a good school and identified some promising housing prospects. But when he pressed Irene to get going on selling their apartment, the result was the worst fight of their marriage. When it became clear that their relationship was being jeopardized, Kipp quit and returned to New York to look for a new job.

The life of a leader is always a balancing act, but never more so than during a transition. The uncertainty and ambiguity can be crippling. You don't even know what you don't know. You haven't had a chance to build a support network. If you have moved, as Kipp Erikson did, you're also in transition personally. If you have a family, they too are in transition. Amid all this turmoil, you are expected to get acclimated quickly and begin to effect positive change in your new organization. For all these reasons, *keeping your balance* is a key transition challenge.

Are you focusing on the right things in the right way? Are you maintaining your energy and keeping your perspective? Are you and your family getting the support you need? As Ron Heifetz put it in *Leadership Without Easy Answers,* "The myth of leadership is the myth of the lone warrior: the solitary individual whose heroism and brilliance enable him to lead the way. . . . [But] even if the weight of carrying people's hopes and pains may fall mainly, for a time, on one person's shoulders, leadership cannot be exercised alone. The lone warrior model of leadership is heroic suicide."[1] So don't try to go it alone.

## Taking Stock

Take a few minutes to complete table 9-1. For each statement, circle the response that best represents your current state of mind.

Now calculate your total score. If it is 25 or higher, or if you circled a 5 in response to any of the statements, you are at risk. Even if your score is below 25, read this chapter anyway.

TABLE 9 - 1

## Balance Assessment

| | Strongly Disagree | Disagree | Neither Agree nor Disagree | Agree | Strongly Agree |
|---|---|---|---|---|---|
| 1. I am very busy, but not finding time for the most important things I ought to be doing. | 1 | 2 | 3 | 4 | 5 |
| 2. I am doing things I should not be doing at the request of others (e.g., my boss, my direct reports). | 1 | 2 | 3 | 4 | 5 |
| 3. I am frustrated that I cannot get things done the way I want them to be done. | 1 | 2 | 3 | 4 | 5 |
| 4. I feel isolated in the organization. | 1 | 2 | 3 | 4 | 5 |
| 5. My judgment seems off these days. | 1 | 2 | 3 | 4 | 5 |
| 6. I am avoiding making tough decisions on key issues (e.g., personnel). | 1 | 2 | 3 | 4 | 5 |
| 7. I have less energy for work than I usually do. | 1 | 2 | 3 | 4 | 5 |

Things may get tougher in the future. This chapter can also help you help others who are struggling with their own transitions.

## Avoiding Vicious Cycles

The seven statements in the table correspond to personal traps into which new leaders can fall. Each of these traps can enmesh you in a *vicious cycle*, a self-reinforcing dynamic from which it will be difficult to escape. It is thus essential to recognize and avoid them. Pay particular attention to those for which you circled a 4 or a 5 in your self-assessment.

1. **Riding off in all directions.** You can't hope to focus others if you can't focus yourself. You can be busy and still fail every single day. Why? Because there is an infinite number of tasks you *could* do during your transition, but only a few that are vital. Perhaps you tell yourself, "If I get enough things going, something has to click," and dissipate your efforts. Perhaps you overestimate your capacity to keep all the balls in the air. Every new leader has to do some parallel processing. But it is easy to reach the point of *mental lock-up*, where you find yourself pulled from task to task faster than you can refocus on each new one. Whatever the explanation, if important problems remain unaddressed, they could explode and suck up more of your time, leaving you even less time, and so on. The result is a vicious cycle of firefighting.

2. **Undefended boundaries.** If you fail to establish solid boundaries defining what you are willing and not

willing to do, the people around you—bosses, peers, and direct reports—will take whatever you have to give. The more you give, the less they will respect you and the more they will ask of you—another vicious cycle. Eventually you will feel angry and resentful that you are being nibbled to death, but you will have no one to blame but yourself. If you cannot establish boundaries for yourself, you cannot expect others to do it for you.

3. **Brittleness.** The uncertainty inherent in transitions breeds rigidity and defensiveness, especially in new leaders with a high need for control. The likely result: overcommitment to a failing course of action. You make a call prematurely and then feel unable to back away from it without losing credibility. The longer you wait, the harder it is to admit you were wrong and the more calamitous the consequences. Or perhaps you decide that your way of accomplishing a particular goal is the only way. As a result your rigidity disempowers people who have equally valid ideas about how to achieve the same goal.

4. **Isolation.**  To be effective, you have to be connected to the people who make action happen and to the subterranean flow of information. It is surprisingly easy for new leaders to end up isolated, and isolation can creep up on you. It happens because you don't take the time to make the right connections, perhaps by relying overmuch on a few people or on "official" information. It also happens if you unintentionally discourage people from sharing critical information with

you. Perhaps they fear your reaction to bad news, or see you as having been captured by competing interests. Whatever the reason, isolation breeds uninformed decision making, which damages your credibility and further reinforces your isolation.

5. **Biased judgment.** Biased judgment—a loss of perspective because of well-recognized weaknesses in human decision making—can take several forms.[2] *Overcommitment* to a failing course of action because of ego and credibility issues is one version. Others include *confirmation bias,* the tendency to focus on information that confirms your beliefs and filter out what does not; *self-serving illusions,* a tendency for your personal stake in a situation to cloud your judgment; and *optimistic overconfidence,* or underestimation of the difficulties associated with your preferred course of action. Vulnerability to these biases is a constant, but you are particularly at risk when the stakes get higher, uncertainty and ambiguity increase, and emotions run high.

6. **Work avoidance.** You will have to make tough calls early in your new job. Perhaps you have to make major decisions about the direction of the business based on incomplete information. Or perhaps your personnel decisions will have a profound impact on people's lives. Consciously or unconsciously, you may choose to delay by burying yourself in other work or fooling yourself that the time isn't ripe to make the call. Ron Heifetz uses the term *work avoidance* to characterize this tendency to avoid taking the bull by the horns, which results in tough problems becoming even tougher.[3]

7. **Going over the top.**  All of these traps can generate
   dangerous levels of stress. Not all stress is bad. In fact,
   there is a well-documented relationship between stress
   and performance known as the Yerkes-Dodson curve,
   illustrated in figure 9-1.[4]

Whether self-generated or externally imposed, you need some
stress (often in the form of positive incentives or consequences
from inaction) to be productive. Without it, not much happens—you stay in bed munching chocolates. As you begin to
experience pressure, your performance improves, at least at
first. Eventually you reach a point (which varies from person to
person) at which further demands, in the form of too many
balls to juggle or too heavy an emotional load, start to undermine performance. This dynamic creates more stress, further
reducing your performance and creating a vicious cycle as you
go over the top of your stress curve. Rarely, outright exhaustion
sets in and the new leader burns out. Much more common is

**FIGURE 9 - 1**

**Yerkes-Dodson Human Performance Curve**

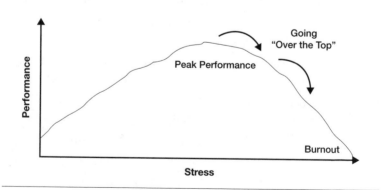

chronic underperformance: You work harder and achieve less. This is what happened to Kipp Erikson.

## The Three Pillars of Self-Efficacy

How can you avoid these traps? How can you create virtuous cycles that build momentum rather than vicious cycles that sap your strength? We will call the equilibrium you should aim for *self-efficacy,* a state that is built on a foundation with three pillars. The first pillar is adoption of the success strategies presented in the previous eight chapters. The second pillar is creation and enforcement of some *personal disciplines.* The third pillar is *support systems,* at work and at home, that help you to maintain your balance.

### Pillar 1: Adopting Success Strategies

The strategies spelled out in the previous eight chapters represent a template for how to learn, set priorities, create plans, and direct action to build momentum. When you see these strategies work and when you get some early successes under your belt, you will feel more confident and energized by what you are accomplishing. As you progress through your transition, think about the challenges you are facing in light of the core challenges summarized in table 9-2 and identify chapters to which you want to return.

### Pillar 2: Enforcing Personal Disciplines

Knowing what you *should* be doing is not the same as doing it. Ultimately, success or failure emerges from the accumulation of

TABLE 9 - 2

## Assessment of Core Challenges

| Core Challenge | Diagnostic Questions |
| --- | --- |
| Promote yourself | Are you adopting the right mind-set for your new job and letting go of the past? |
| Accelerate your learning | Are you figuring out what you need to learn, from whom to learn it, and how to speed up the learning process? |
| Match strategy to situation | Are you diagnosing the type of transition you are facing and the implications for what to do and what not to do? |
| Secure early wins | Are you focusing on the vital priorities that advance long-term goals and build short-term momentum? |
| Negotiate success | Are you building your relationship with your new boss, managing expectations, and marshaling the resources you need? |
| Achieve alignment | Are you identifying and fixing frustrating misalignments of strategy, structure, systems, and skills? |
| Build your team | Are you assessing, restructuring, and aligning your team to leverage what you are trying to accomplish? |
| Create coalitions | Are you building a base of internal and external support for your initiatives so you are not pushing rocks uphill? |

daily choices that propel you in productive directions or push you off a cliff. This is the territory of the second pillar of personal efficacy: personal disciplines.

Personal disciplines are the regular routines that you enforce on yourself ruthlessly. What specific disciplines are the highest priorities for you to develop? It depends on what your strengths and weaknesses are. You may have a great deal of insight into yourself, but you should also consult others who know you well and whom you trust. (Some 360-degree feedback can be useful here.) What do they see as your strengths and, crucially, your potential weak spots?

This list of personal disciplines can stimulate your thinking about routines you need to develop.

***Plan to Plan.***    Do you devote time daily and weekly to a plan-work-evaluate cycle? If not, or if you do so irregularly, you need to be more disciplined about planning. At the end of each day, spend ten minutes evaluating how well you met the goals you set the previous day and planning for the next day. Do the same at the end of each week. Get into the habit of doing this. Even if you fall behind, you will be more in control.

***Judiciously Defer Commitment.***    Do you make commitments on the spur of the moment and regret them later? Do you blithely agree to do things in the seemingly remote future, only to kick yourself when the day arrives and your schedule is full? If so, you have to learn to defer commitment. Anytime anybody asks you to do something, say, "Sounds interesting. Let me think about it and get back to you." Never say yes on the spot. If you are being pressed (perhaps by someone who knows your vulnerability to such pressure), say, "Well, if you need an answer now, I'll have to say no. But if you can wait, I will give it more thought." Begin with no; it is easy to say yes later. It is difficult (and damaging to your reputation) to say yes and then change your mind. Keep in mind that people will ask you to make commitments far in advance, knowing that your schedule will look deceptively open. Ask yourself, as my former colleague Robert Robinson so aptly put it, whether "future you" will hate "present you" for saying yes. If the answer is yes, say no.

***Set Aside Time for the Hard Work.***    Do you devote time each day to the most important work that needs to be done? It is easy to get caught up in the flow of transactions—phone calls, meetings, e-mail—and never find time to focus on the medium term, let alone the long run. If you are having trouble getting the real work done, discipline yourself to set aside a particular time each day, even as little as half an hour, when you will close the door, shut off the phone, ignore e-mail, and focus, focus, focus.

*Go to the Balcony.*   Do you find yourself getting too caught up in the emotional dimension of difficult situations? If so, discipline yourself to stand back from difficult situations, take stock from 50,000 feet, and then make productive interventions. Leading authorities in the fields of leadership and negotiation have long praised the value of "going to the balcony" in this way.[5] It can be tough to do this, especially when the stakes are high and you are emotionally involved. But with discipline and practice, it is a skill that can be cultivated.

*Focus on Process.*   Do you have good ideas but consistently find that you alienate others in trying to implement them? Does the way you make decisions cause unnecessary dissension and disagreement? If so, discipline yourself to focus on *influence process design* before plunging ahead. Think: How are others likely to react to your ideas? How might you manage the process of consultation and decision making to increase your effectiveness? Remember: People will often go along with things they are not completely happy about if they perceive the process as fair.[6]

*Check in with Yourself.*   Are you as aware as you need to be of your reactions to events during your transition? If not, discipline yourself to engage in structured reflection about your situation. For some new leaders, structured self-assessment means jotting down a few thoughts, impressions, and questions at the end of

## Guidelines for Structured Reflection

The power of structured reflection is heightened if you pursue it regularly and are attentive to how your responses change over time. Consider setting aside fifteen minutes at the end of each week to answer the same set of questions. Save your responses so you can look back regularly at the preceding couple of weeks. You will see patterns develop, both in the nature of the problems you face and in your reactions to them.

### What do you feel so far?

On a scale of high to low, do you feel:

- Excited? If not, why not? What can you do about it?
- Confident? If not, why not? What can you do about it?
- In control of your success? If not, why not? What can you do about it?

### What has bothered you so far?

- With whom have you failed to connect? Why?
- Of the meetings you have attended, which has been the most troubling? Why?
- Of all that you have seen or heard, what has disturbed you most? Why?

### What has gone well or poorly?

- Which interactions would you handle differently if you could? Which exceeded your expectations? Why?
- Which of your decisions have turned out particularly well? Not so well? Why?

*(continued)*

**Guidelines for Structured Reflection** *(continued)*

- What missed opportunities do you regret most? Was a better result blocked primarily by you or by something beyond your control?

Now focus on the biggest challenges or difficulties you are facing. Be honest with yourself. Are your difficulties situational or do their sources lie within you? Even experienced and skilled people blame problems on the situation rather than their own actions. The net effect is that they are less proactive than they could be.

---

each day. For others it means setting aside time each week to assess how things are going. Find an approach that suits your style, and discipline yourself to use it regularly. Work to translate the resulting insights into action. Consider adopting the guidelines for self-reflection listed in the accompanying box.

*Recognize When to Quit.*    To adapt an old saw, transitions are marathons, not sprints. If you find yourself going over the top of your stress curve more than occasionally, you have to discipline yourself to know when to quit. This is easy to say and hard to do, of course, especially when you are up against a deadline and one more hour might make all the difference. It may, in the short run, but the long-run cost could be steep. Work hard at recognizing when you are at the point of diminishing returns and take a break of whatever sort refreshes you.

### Pillar 3: Building Your Support Systems

The first two pillars of self-efficacy are systematic planning and disciplined execution; the third is solidifying your personal support systems. This means asserting control in your local environment, stabilizing the home front, and building a solid advice-and-counsel network.

***Assert Control Locally.***    It is hard to focus on work if the basic infrastructure that supports you is not in place. Even if you have more pressing worries, move quickly to get your new office set up, develop routines, and clarify expectations with your assistant, and so on. If necessary, assemble a set of temporary resources—files, references, information technology, and staff support—to tide you over until the permanent systems are operational.

***Stabilize the Home Front.***    It is a fundamental rule of warfare to avoid fighting on too many fronts. For new leaders, this means stabilizing the home front so you can devote the necessary attention to work. You cannot hope to create value at work if you are destroying value at home. This is the fundamental mistake that Kipp Erikson made.

If your new position involves relocation, your family is also in transition. Like Irene Erikson, your spouse may be making a job transition too, and your children may have to leave their friends and change schools. In other words, the fabric of your family's life may be disrupted just when you most need support and stability. The stresses of your professional transition can amplify the strain of your family's transition. Also, family members' difficulties can add to your already heavy emotional load, undermining your ability to create value and lengthening the time it takes for you to reach the breakeven point.

So focus on accelerating the family transition too. The starting point is to acknowledge that your family may be unhappy, even resentful, about the transition. There is no avoiding disruption, but talking about it and working through the sense of loss together can be helpful.

Beyond that, here are some guidelines that can help to smooth your family's transition:

- **Analyze your family's existing support system.** Moving severs your ties with the people who provide essential services for your family: doctors, lawyers, dentists, babysitters, tutors, coaches, and more. Do an inventory, identify priorities, and invest in finding replacements quickly.

- **Get your spouse back on track.** Your spouse may quit his or her old job with the intention of finding a new one after relocating. Unhappiness can fester if the search is slow. To accelerate it, negotiate up front with your company for job-search support or find such support shortly after moving. Above all, don't let your spouse defer getting going.

- **Time the family move carefully.** For children, it is substantially more difficult to move in the middle of a school year. Consider waiting until the end of the school year to move your family. The price, of course, is separation from your loved ones and the wear and tear of commuting. If you do this, however, be sure that your spouse has extra support to help ease the burden. Being a single parent is hard work.

- **Preserve the familiar.** Reestablish familiar family rituals as quickly as possible and maintain them throughout the transition. Help from favorite relatives, such as grandparents, also makes a difference.

- **Invest in cultural familiarization.** If you move interna-
  tionally, get professional advice about the cross-cultural
  transition. Isolation is a far greater risk for your family
  if there are language and cultural barriers.

- **Tap into your company's relocation service, if it has one,
  as soon as possible.** Corporate relocation services are
  typically limited to helping you find a new home, move
  belongings, and locate schools, but such help can
  make a big difference.

There is no avoiding pain if you decide to move your family.
But there is much you can do to minimize it and to accelerate
everyone's transitions.

*Build your Advice-and-Counsel Network.*   No leader, no matter
how capable and energetic, can do it all. You need a network of
trusted advisers within and outside the organization with whom
to talk through what you are experiencing. Your network is an
indispensable resource that can help you avoid becoming isolated and losing perspective. As a starting point, you need to
cultivate three types of advice givers: technical advisers, cultural
interpreters, and political counselors (see table 9-3).

You also need to think hard about the mix of internal and
external advice-givers you want to cultivate. Insiders know the
organization, its culture and politics. Seek out people who are
well connected and who you can trust to help you grasp what is
really going on. They are a priceless resource.

At the same time, insiders cannot be expected to give you dispassionate or disinterested views of events. Thus, you should
augment your internal network with outside advisers and counselors who will help you work through the issues and decisions

TABLE 9 - 3

## Types of Advice Givers

| Type | Roles | How They Help You |
|---|---|---|
| Technical advisers | Provide expert analysis of technologies, markets, and strategy | They suggest applications for new technologies. They recommend strategies for entering new markets. They provide timely and accurate information. |
| Cultural interpreters | Help you understand the new culture and (if that is your objective) to adapt to it | They provide you with insight into cultural norms, mental models, and guiding assumptions. They help you learn to speak the language of the new organization. |
| Political counselors | Help you deal with political relationships within your new organization | They help you implement the advice of your technical advisers. They serve as a sounding board as you think through options for implementing your agenda. They challenge you with what-if questions. |

you are facing. They should be skilled at listening and asking questions, have good insight into the way organizations work, and have your best interests at heart.

Use table 9-4 to assess your advice-and-counsel network. Analyze each person in terms of the domains in which they assist you and whether they are insiders and outsiders.

Now take a step back. Will your existing network provide the support you need in your new situation? Don't assume that people who have been helpful in the past will continue to be helpful in your new situation. You will encounter different problems, and former advisers may not be able to help you in your new role. As you attain higher levels of responsibility, for example, the need for good political counsel increases dramatically.

TABLE 9 - 4

## Assessment of Your Advice-and-Counsel Network

|  | Technical Advisers | Cultural Interpreters | Political Counselors |
|---|---|---|---|
| **Internal Advisers and Counselors (inside your new organization)** |  |  |  |
| **External Advisers and Counselors (outside your new organization)** |  |  |  |

You should also be thinking ahead. Because it takes time to develop an effective network, it's not too early to focus on what sort of network you will need in your *next* job. How will your needs for advice change?

To develop an effective support network, you need to make sure that you have the right help and that your support network is there when you need it. Does your support network have the following qualities?

- The right mix of technical advisers, cultural inter-preters, and political counselors.

- The right mix of internal and external advice-givers. You want honest feedback from insiders *and* the dispassionate perspective of outside observers.

- External supporters who are loyal to you as an individual, not to your new organization or unit. Typically, these are long-standing colleagues and friends.

- Internal advisers who are trustworthy, whose personal agendas don't conflict with yours, and who offer straight and accurate advice.

- Representatives of key constituencies who can help you understand their perspectives. You do not want to restrict yourself to one or two points of view.

## Staying on Track

You will have to fight to keep your balance every single day. Ultimately, your success or failure will flow from all the small choices you make along the way. These choices can create momentum—for the organization and for you—or they can result in death by a thousand cuts. Your day-to-day actions during your transition establish the pattern for all that follows, not just for the organization but also for your personal efficacy and ultimately your well-being.

### ACCELERATION CHECKLIST

1. What are your greatest vulnerabilities in your new job? How do you plan to compensate for them?

2. What personal disciplines do you most need to develop or enhance? How will you do that? What will success look like?

3. What can you do to gain more control over your local environment?

4. What can you do to ease your family's transition? What support relationships will you have to build? Which are your highest priorities?

5. What are your priorities for strengthening your advice-and-counsel network? To what extent do you need to focus on your internal network? Your external network? In which domain do you most need additional support: technical, political, or personal?

# 10

# Expedite Everyone

THE STRATEGIES laid out in the preceding chapters should propel you on your way to reaping the rewards of a stunningly successful transition. But that doesn't mean you are done. What about your direct reports and their direct reports? Don't you have a stake in the success of their transitions?

In doing the research for this book, I set out to solve a mystery. Why do so few companies make it an organizational priority to accelerate the transitions of their managers? To put it another way, why wouldn't companies try to capture the potential benefits of speeding up everyone's transitions? Roughly 25 percent of the managers in a typical company take new jobs each year, and each person in transition affects many others. So it is surprising how few companies pay attention to accelerating transitions. A few companies (GE, for example) explicitly teach their managers how to accelerate their transitions. More common are "assimilation" programs that introduce outside hires to the strategy, businesses, and culture of the company. Although useful, such programs seldom provide guidance on systematically managing the *process* of a successful transition. The vast majority of companies do not provide any support at all.

Why is this the case? Part of the explanation lies in changes in leadership development. The flattening of hierarchies and the faster pace of business have shrunk the amount of time line managers can devote to developing and counseling their direct reports, including during critical transition periods. To compensate, professional education-and-development units have assumed increasing responsibility for leadership development. The result has been significant advances in the development of "hard" skills. But the price has been a dramatic reduction in the transfer of managerial wisdom from senior managers to their less experienced counterparts, particularly regarding "soft" skills like how to take charge in a new role.

"Sink-or-swim" managerial culture is a second barrier. Many companies treat transitions as a way of winnowing talent—an approach I call *Darwinian leadership development*. Promising managers are dumped into the deep end of the pool to test their evolutionary fitness for advancement. The swimmers are deemed to have high potential, and the sinkers . . . sink. In some organizations, this process verges on hazing: As we have suffered, so shall ye. One senior executive said to me, without a trace of irony, "You're not going to make this [transitioning] too easy for them, are you?" As if that were possible. In particularly dysfunctional organizations, competing factions even maneuver unwary up-and-comers into roles in which they will fail and so end up out of the running for more senior positions.

That said, there is no question that transitions are a key element of a comprehensive approach to leadership development. Recall that in McKinsey & Company's 1998 "war for talent" survey, the types of experiences considered the "most important for development" all involved transitions. The top three were a new position with large scope, turning around a business, and starting a new business.[1] However, developing leaders does not mean sending them into challenging situations unprepared. A fundamental flaw in the Darwinian approach to leadership development is that there are many kinds of transitions, and therefore the lessons younger managers learn may not equip them for the next level or for a new type of business situation. The result? Some high-potential people make early mistakes and drown. Others swim, but only because they end up in the right kind of position or have the right lifeguard looking out for them.

Organizations are not well served in the long run by unregulated Darwinian leadership development. It's like the free market run amok, without the safeguards provided by rules and regulations. The best companies definitely are meritocracies. Their leaders compete to rise to the top and continually reinvigorate the enterprise. But true meritocracies start with a level playing field. People succeed because they have the right stuff and not because they get placed in situations that happen to be good matches to their skills.

The tenth and final challenge, therefore, is to *expedite everyone* by institutionalizing the transition acceleration model presented in this book. If *all* the leaders who take on new positions in your organization use these success strategies, you will not just prevent failures, you will also capture potentially massive gains from accelerating everyone. The faster everyone settles in, the faster the organization can begin to make the right moves to gain market share, cut costs, and launch more new products.

Think about it. What would it be worth in bottom-line terms if you could get everyone in your organization—your new direct reports, their new direct reports, and so on—to the breakeven point just 5 percent faster?

## Creating a Common Language

Suppose you wanted to introduce the transition acceleration framework in your organization. How might you best do it? The starting point is to introduce a new vocabulary for talking about transitions. This probably is the single most important step your organization can take to institutionalize transition acceleration. Imagine that every time anyone made a transition into a new leadership role, he or she was able to talk with bosses, peers, and direct reports about the following:

- The type of transition they were in, using the $ST_ARS$ model—start-up, turnaround, realignment, or sustaining success—and the associated challenges and opportunities

- Their agenda for technical, cultural, and political learning and the key elements of their learning plan

- Their progress in engaging their new boss in the five conversations about situation, expectations, style, resources, and personal development

- Their A-item priorities, goals for behavior change, and ideas for where they would secure early wins

- Their priorities for strengthening their advice-and-counsel network

A common language makes discussions of these issues dramatically more efficient. Perhaps more important, it means that conversations will happen that wouldn't have happened otherwise. It also makes people more forthcoming, more likely to share confidences and information, and more tolerant of others' transition struggles. This helps move the organization beyond "sink or swim."

Anyone who has tried to institutionalize new ideas in an organization can tell you that it's an uphill battle. So begin by working locally. Focus on the people who work for you, both new direct reports and people who have been around for a while.

When you next hire new direct reports, experiment with how quickly you can get them to the breakeven point. Press them to create their own 90-day acceleration plan. Start by introducing them to the five-conversations framework for building a relationship with their new boss—you. Then have them diagnose the business situation and discuss it with you, initiating the situation conversation. Merge this with the expectations conversation. Now work with them to create a learning agenda and learning plan. Help them identify and reach out to people whose support they are likely to need. Press them on their A-item priorities and plans for securing early wins. Once you get them up to speed, press them to use the transition acceleration framework with their own people.

In parallel with this, choose a direct report who has been around for a while and who you believe to be open-minded. Experiment with helping him or her to accelerate his or her people. Put this individual in the role of teacher, which is often the best way to learn something new. See how far down you can cascade the framework.

## Working with a Team

If you are building a team, consider using the framework to accelerate the team-building process. One virtue of the transition acceleration model is that it supplies the team with a common language for talking about shared challenges. This can be especially powerful if your team mixes people who have been around for a while with people transitioning into new roles. By introducing a new framework and language, you level the playing field between the old guard and the new.

Start by providing your team an overview of the transition acceleration framework. Then focus the team on doing a shared situational diagnosis using the $ST_ARS$ model. Push them to clarify the key challenges and opportunities. Then move onto alignment issues—strategy, structure, systems, and skills. Next, focus on how the team will define its A-item priorities and secure early wins. Finally, explore the kinds of coalitions you and the team will have to build to marshal the support you need.

## Bringing in People from Outside

Healthy organizations bring in people from outside, ideally midlevel people, to seed new ideas and energy. But few organizations do a good job of helping outsiders become insiders. As a result, promising people make unnecessary mistakes, often in the spheres of organizational culture and politics.

How do you avoid this? Get them to create their own 90-day acceleration plan. Start by using the $ST_ARS$ model to identify the jobs that are appropriate for outside hires. Don't set them up to fail, such as by putting them in a realignment situation without adequate support and advice. Teach them the same transition acceleration vocabulary that insiders speak so they can converse easily about, for example, what is considered a "win" in your organization. Develop a primer about the company culture, perhaps a video of leaders who have successfully transitioned in from the outside talking about what works and what doesn't.

## Developing High-Potential Leaders

An executive-development program based on the transition acceleration model can be a central component of a more ambitious strategy for developing high-potential leaders. In such programs, which typically last days, cohorts of high-potential leaders who are transitioning into new roles are introduced to the transition acceleration model, work through new-leader simulations and case studies, and do some first-90-days planning for their own transitions. In the course of intense work in small groups, longer-term advice-and-counsel relationships often coalesce.

## Strengthening Succession Planning

Effective succession-planning systems call for (1) rigorous evaluation of leadership potential and (2) thoughtful design of developmental pathways for high-potential leaders. Good systems foster cross-functional expertise and help to groom the company's future general managers. In global companies, they expose up-and-coming managers to international experience early in their careers. Increasingly, they also factor critical career breakpoints or passages into the development equation.

But most existing systems fall short, in both evaluation and development, because they lack a framework for characterizing developmental assignments. Without such a framework, it is problematic to make comparisons between high-potential individuals placed in dissimilar situations. Succession planners also lack a way of describing—and thus managing—the sequence of positions through which high-potential leaders progress.

Succession planning can be strengthened substantially by looking not just at the people, but also at the transitions—start-ups, turnarounds, realignments, and sustaining-success situations—they have experienced. The $ST_ARS$ model provides a basis for evaluating performance in very different types of situations. Perhaps more important, it provides a basis for charting the progression of high-potential leaders through a series of positions that build their capability to manage a broad range of business situations.

To illustrate, think of your own job history. Take some time to fill out the *development grid,* a tool for charting professional development shown in table 10-1. The rows represent functions in which you have worked, and the columns represent types of business situations you have experienced.

Chart every management position you have held, plus any major project or task force assignments. For example, if your first managerial job was in marketing in an organization (or unit) in the midst of a turnaround, place a circled 1 (indicating your first management position) in the corresponding cell of the matrix. If your next position was in sales in a new unit (or dealing with a new product or project)—a start-up situation—enter a circled 2 in that cell. If at the same time you were on a task force dealing with operations issues for the start-up, enter a 2 inside a triangle (indicating a project assignment) in the appropriate cell.

Record all your managerial jobs, and then connect the dots to illuminate your professional trajectory. Are there any blank columns or rows? What do they signify about your readiness for general-management positions? About your potential blind spots?

As discussed previously, preparing people to manage different types of business situations constitutes a fourth dimension of leadership development that complements analyses

TABLE 10 - 1

## The Development Grid

| | Start-up | Turnaround | Realignment | Sustaining Success |
|---|---|---|---|---|
| Marketing | | | | |
| Sales | | | | |
| Finance | | | | |
| Human Resources | | | | |
| Operations | | | | |
| R&D | | | | |
| Information Management | | | | |
| Other | | | | |

of (1) breadth of functional expertise, (2) extent of international experience, (3) and key passages between levels in the organization.

## Accelerating Postmerger Integration

The transition acceleration model has also been used successfully as a driver of postmerger integration, during which many people are in transition simultaneously. Its impact goes beyond accelerating individual managers into their new positions, however.

When organizations collide, the two populations effectively start out speaking different languages. Culture clashes are often as much about language as they are about values. Misunderstandings generate conflict, which undermines the integration process. The transition acceleration model is a new language that both organizations can learn together.

## Employing Performance-Support Tools

Finally, you might consider using Harvard Business School Publishing's online performance-support tool, Leadership Transitions (www.harvardbusinessonline.com), as a resource for introducing the transition acceleration model into your organization. You can make the tool available via the Web to everyone in your organization, regardless how geographically decentralized. The tool provides a wealth of supporting diagnostics and tools that new leaders can use on a just-in-time basis to accelerate their transitions. The tool was deliberately designed not as a course but as a flexible performance-support resource that new leaders can draw on when they need it. Thus, you can employ efficient blended approaches to cascade the model down through an organization. A typical configuration is an initial short (half-day maximum) face-to-face or Web conference introduction to the transition acceleration model and the online performance-support tool.

### ACCELERATION CHECKLIST

1. Whose transitions would you most like to accelerate? How might you begin?

2. Would a structured new-leader assimilation process help to accelerate you and your new team?

3. What can you do to better support the transitions of people who come in from the outside?

4. Should transition acceleration be part of your organization's curriculum for developing high-potential leaders? How might different types of business situations be factored into succession planning?

5. Could the transition acceleration model help smooth the integration of acquisitions?

6. Can you leverage the transition acceleration model through adoption of an online performance-support tool?

# Conclusion:
# Beyond Sink
# or Swim

THE GOAL OF THIS BOOK is to move you—and your organization—beyond the sink-or-swim approach to managing transitions. If you apply the strategies laid out in the previous ten chapters systematically, you will dramatically accelerate your ability to move into new roles and reach the breakeven point. The people who work for you likewise stand to benefit greatly if you help them to be more methodical in their approaches to transition acceleration. And the faster they get up to speed, the more they can help you achieve your goals.

My goal in highlighting the ten key transition challenges, and in presenting techniques for surmounting them, is to help you develop your situational awareness and augment your toolbox. Having spent a lot of time focusing on the trees, then, it is appropriate to step back and take a look at the forest as a whole.

At the beginning of the book, I laid out five core propositions concerning transitions and what it takes to be effective in meeting them. Let us conclude by taking a fresh look at them:

1. **The root causes of transition failure always lie in a pernicious interaction between the situation, with its opportunities and pitfalls, and the individual, with his or her strengths and vulnerabilities.** Your success or failure rests, to no small degree, on your ability to diagnose your situation, identify its characteristic challenges and opportunities, and fashion promising action plans. If you don't understand the demands of the situation, you will underperform or even fail outright. Coupled with an understanding of your own strengths and weaknesses, thorough situational diagnosis will help you pinpoint vulnerabilities so you can take preventive actions.

2. **There are systematic methods that leaders can employ to both lessen the likelihood of failure and reach the breakeven point faster.** The difference between transitioning into a lower-level management position and becoming CEO is more a matter of degree than of kind. Of course, senior managers must address issues (such as organizational alignment, building a top team, and managing external constituencies) that are outside the purview of lower-level managers. But most of the basic imperatives—promote yourself, match strategy to your situation, accelerate your learning, secure early wins, create coalitions—apply at all levels, as do the fundamental tools and planning guidelines. The overarching imperative, in all transitions, is to find ways to create value sooner and so reach the

breakeven point more quickly. The value of putting together a 90-day plan is great regardless of your level.

3. **The overriding goal in a transition is to build momentum by creating virtuous cycles that build credibility and by avoiding getting caught in vicious cycles that damage credibility.** Leadership is ultimately about leverage. Effective leaders leverage themselves—their ideas, energy, relationships, and influence—to create new patterns in organizations. The leader is just one person, and one person can accomplish very little alone. The ability to leverage oneself rests in turn on perceptions of personal credibility and demonstrated effectiveness. This is how small successes yield leadership capital that can be invested to yield larger returns. The underlying goal of the strategies presented in this book—whether getting early wins, creating coalitions, or building the team—is to help new leaders build momentum, and thus increase their leverage.

4. **Transitions are a crucible for leadership development and should be managed accordingly.** I hope this book has convinced you that Darwinian leadership development wastes time, energy, and talent. You should certainly use transitions into demanding new positions to challenge your up-and-coming leaders. But don't just leave them to sink or swim. Teach them the transition acceleration skills they need to have a fighting chance. By leveling the playing field, you will also be better able to discern whose abilities really stand out.

5. **Successful adoption of a standard framework for accelerating transitions can yield big returns for organizations.**

Take the time to figure out how many people transition into new management roles in your organization in a typical year. Then estimate how many others each transitioning manager affects. What would you estimate as the net annual cost of transition in your organization? What would it be worth to reduce that cost by just 5 percent? Keeping people in jobs longer, as attractive as that might seem, is not the answer. Good people get bored after a few years and yearn for new challenges. The best approach is to help everyone in your organization to accelerate every transition.

If you are an experienced leader, you almost certainly are already using some of the approaches you encountered in the pages of this book. You may have said to yourself, "Aha, that's what I was doing!" But some of your beliefs about what it takes to succeed in a new job should also have been reworked and refined. The biggest danger you face is belief in one-size-fits-all rules for success.

If you are still in an early stage of your career as a manager, you have many lessons yet to learn, but you haven't picked up many bad habits either. You can get it right from the start. And you can work on honing your skills through the many transitions you will experience in the future.

# Notes

## Introduction

1. Analysis of data from survey of participants in Harvard Business School's 2003 YPO President's Seminar and 2003 WPO/CEO Seminar.

2. Excellent exceptions to this general rule are John J. Gabarro, *The Dynamics of Taking Charge* (Boston: Harvard Business School Press, 1987) and Linda A. Hill, *Becoming a Manager: How New Managers Master the Challenges of Leadership*, 2d ed. (Boston: Harvard Business School Press, 2003).

3. For an excellent exploration of the challenges of moving from technical contributor to first-time manager, see Hill, *Becoming a Manager*.

4. Helen Handfield-Jones, "How Executives Grow," *McKinsey Quarterly* 1 (2000): 121.

5. This is an extrapolation of the results of a management transition survey of senior HR executives at *Fortune* 500 companies that I conducted in 1999. The survey was sent to the heads of human resources at a random sample of 100 *Fortune* 500 companies. We received 40 responses. One question concerned the percentage of managers at all levels who took new jobs in 1998. The mean of the responses to this question was 22.3 percent. Extrapolated to the *Fortune* 500 as a whole, this suggests that almost 700,000 managers take new jobs each year. The half-million figure is therefore a conservative estimate intended purely to illustrate the magnitude of the impact of leadership transitions.

6. Results are from the 1999 management transition survey that was sent to the heads of human resources at a random sample of 100 *Fortune* 500 companies (see previous note).

241

7. Analysis of data from survey of participants in Harvard Business School's 2003 YPO President's Seminar and 2003 WPO/CEO Seminar.

8. Results of a study by the Center for Creative Leadership, as cited in *Fortune* magazine. See Anne Fisher, "Don't Blow Your New Job," *Fortune,* 22 June 1998. Brad Smart estimated the mishire rate to be over 50 percent. See Brad Smart, *Topgrading: How Leading Companies Win by Hiring, Coaching, and Keeping the Best People* (Upper Saddle River, NJ: Prentice Hall, 1999), 47.

9. This estimate comes from Brad Smart, *Topgrading,* 46. Smart, a leading HR consultant, conducted a study that estimated the cost of a failed hire to be 24 times base compensation, assuming a base compensation of $114,000.

10. Data from 1999 management transition survey of heads of HR at *Fortune* 500 companies.

11. For a discussion of key passages in the lives of managers, see Ram Charan, Stephen Drotter, and James Noel, *The Leadership Pipeline: How to Build the Leadership-Powered Company* (San Francisco: Jossey-Bass, 2001).

## Chapter 1

1. Ivester's story is chronicled in M. Watkins, C. Knoop, and C. Reavis, "The Coca-Cola Co. (A): The Rise and Fall of M. Douglas Ivester," Case 9-800-355 (Boston: Harvard Business School, 2000).

2. C. Mitchell, "Challenges Await Coca-Cola's New Leader," *Atlanta Journal and Constitution,* 27 October 1997.

3. P. Sellars, "Where Coke Goes from Here," *Fortune,* 13 October 1997.

4. "Clumsy Handling of Many Problems Cost Ivester Coca-Cola Board's Favor," *Wall Street Journal,* 17 December 1999.

5. Chris Argyris, "Teaching Smart People How to Learn," *Harvard Business Review,* May–June 1991.

6. See Ronald Heifetz, *Leadership Without Easy Answers* (Cambridge, MA: Belknap Press, 1994).

## Chapter 2

1. For an informative exploration of organizational culture and the role of leaders in shaping it, see Edgar Schein, *Organizational Culture and Leadership,* 2d ed. (San Francisco: Jossey-Bass, 1992).

2. Geri Augusto, unpublished presentations to executive programs at the Kennedy School of Government and the Harvard Business School, Boston, MA.

## Chapter 3

1. See Ram Charan, Stephen Drotter, and James Noel, *The Leadership Pipeline: How to Build the Leadership-Powered Company* (San Francisco: Jossey-Bass, 2001).

## Chapter 4

1. See Dan Ciampa and Michael Watkins, "Securing Early Wins," chapter 2 in *Right from the Start: Taking Charge in a New Leadership Role* (Boston: Harvard Business School Press, 1999).

2. Stephen Leacock, *Laugh with Leacock: An Anthology of the Best Work of Stephen Leacock* (New York: Dodd, Mead, 1981).

3. See John J. Gabarro, *The Dynamics of Taking Charge* (Boston: Harvard Business School Press, 1987). This is a wonderful study of the transitions of general managers.

4. See Michael Watkins and Max Bazerman, "Predictable Surprises: The Disasters You Should Have Seen Coming," *Harvard Business Review,* March 2003.

5. My colleague Amy Edmondson developed this very useful distinction.

## Chapter 6

1. This is an adaptation of the well-known McKinsey "7-S" organizational analysis framework. See R. H. Waterman, T. J. Peters, and J. R. Phillips, "Structure Is Not Organization," *Business Horizons,* 1980. For an overview, see "Organizational Alignment: The 7-S Model," Case 9-497-045 (Boston: Harvard Business School, 1996). The seven S's are strategy, structure, systems, staffing, skills, style, and shared values.

2. The SWOT framework was originally described in the late 1960s by Edmund P. Learned, C. Roland Christiansen, Kenneth Andrews, and William D. Guth in *Business Policy: Text and Cases* (Homewood, IL: Irwin, 1969).

3. For an in-depth exploration of these issues, see Michael C. Jensen, *Foundations of Organizational Strategy* (Cambridge: Harvard University Press, 1998).

4. Building "ambidextrous" organizations that can do both of these well is a challenge. See Michael L. Tushman and Charles O'Reilly III, *Winning Through Innovation: A Practical Guide to Leading Organizational Change and Renewal,* rev. ed. (Boston: Harvard Business School Press, 2002).

## Chapter 7

1. Our work has focused on how the leaders of senior teams can more effectively manage decision making. The first fruits of this collaboration are

contained in A. Edmondson, M. Roberto, and M. Watkins, "A Dynamic Model of Top Management Team Effectiveness: Managing Unstructured Task Streams," *Leadership Quarterly* 14, no. 3 (Spring 2003).

2. For a discussion of the importance of perception of fairness in process, see W. Chan Kim and Renée A. Mauborgne, "Fair Process: Managing in the Knowledge Economy," *Harvard Business Review*, July–August 1997.

## Chapter 8

1. See D. Krackhardt and J. R. Hanson, "Informal Networks: The Company Behind the Chart," *Harvard Business Review*, July–August 1993.

2. David Lax and Jim Sebenius coined this term. See David Lax and James Sebenius, "Thinking Coalitionally," in *Negotiation Analysis*, ed. H. Peyton Young (Ann Arbor: University of Michigan Press, 1991), and James Sebenius, "Sequencing to Build Coalitions: With Whom Should I Talk First?" in *Wise Choices: Decisions, Games, and Negotiations*, ed. Richard J. Zeckhauser, Ralph L. Keeney, and James K. Sebenius (Boston: Harvard Business School Press, 1996).

## Chapter 9

1. See Ronald Heifetz, *Leadership Without Easy Answers* (Cambridge, MA: Belknap Press, 1994), 251.

2. For an in-depth exploration of managerial biases, see Max Bazerman, *Judgment in Managerial Decision Making*, 5th ed. (New York: Wiley, 2001).

3. See Heifetz, *Leadership Without Easy Answers*.

4. This was originally developed as a model of anxiety. See R. M. Yerkes and J. D. Dodson, "The Relation of Strength of Stimulus to Rapidity of Habit Formation," *Journal of Comparative Neurology and Psychology* 18 (1908): 459–482. Naturally, this model has limitations and is most useful as a metaphor. For a discussion of limitations, see "How Useful Is the Human Function Curve?" at http://www.trance.dircon.co.uk/curve.html.

5. For a discussion of "going to the balcony" in the context of negotiation, see chapter 1 of William Ury, *Getting Past No: Negotiating Your Way from Confrontation to Cooperation* (New York: Bantam Doubleday, 1993).

6. W. Chan Kim and Renée A. Mauborgne, "Fair Process: Managing in the Knowledge Economy," *Harvard Business Review*, July–August 1997.

## Chapter 10

1. Helen Handfield-Jones, "How Executives Grow," *McKinsey Quarterly* 1 (2000).

# Recommended Reading

## Crafting Strategy

Brandenberger, Adam, and Barry Nalebuff. *Co-opetition*. New York: Doubleday, 1996.

Ghemawat, Pankaj, with David J. Collis, Gary P. Pisano, and Jan W. Rivkin. *Strategy and the Business Landscape*. Reading, MA: Addison-Wesley, 1999.

Porter, Michael. *On Competition*. Boston: Harvard Business School Press, 1998.

Watkins, Michael, Mickey Edwards, and Usha Thakrar. *Winning the Influence Game: What Every Business Leader Should Know About Government*. New York: Wiley, 2001.

## Designing Organizations

Kaplan, Robert S., and David P. Norton. *The Strategy-Focused Organization: How Balanced Scorecard Companies Thrive in the New Business Environment*. Boston: Harvard Business School Press, 2001.

Nadler, David, and Michael L. Tushman, with Mark B. Nadler. *Competing by Design: The Power of Organizational Architecture*. New York: Oxford University Press, 1997.

## Managing Change

Kotter, John P. *Leading Change*. Boston: Harvard Business School Press, 1996.

Schein, Edgar H. *Organizational Culture and Leadership*. 2d ed. San Francisco: Jossey-Bass, 1992.

Tushman, Michael L., and Charles O'Reilly III. *Winning Through Innovation: A*

*Practical Guide to Leading Organizational Change and Renewal.* Rev. ed. Boston: Harvard Business School Press, 2002.

## Negotiating and Persuading

Cialdini, Robert. *Influence: The Psychology of Persuasion.* Rev. ed. New York: Morrow, 1993.

Stone, Douglas, Bruce Patton, and Sheila Heen. *Difficult Conversations: How to Discuss What Matters Most.* New York: Viking, 1999.

Ury, William. *Getting Past No: Negotiating Your Way from Confrontation to Cooperation.* New York: Bantam Doubleday, 1993.

Watkins, Michael. *Breakthrough Business Negotiation: A Toolbox for Managers.* San Francisco: Jossey-Bass, 2002.

## Leading and Team Building

Bazerman, Max. *Judgment in Managerial Decision Making.* 5th ed. New York: Wiley, 2002.

Heifetz, Ronald A., and Marty Linsky. *Leadership on the Line: Staying Alive Through the Dangers of Leading.* Boston: Harvard Business School Press, 2002.

Hill, Linda A., *Becoming a Manager: How New Managers Master the Challenges of Leadership,* 2nd ed. Boston: Harvard Business School Press, 2003.

Katzenbach, Jon R., and Douglas K. Smith. *The Wisdom of Teams: Creating the High-Performance Organization.* Boston: Harvard Business School Press, 1993.

# Index

# About the Author

*Michael Watkins* is an Associate Professor at Harvard Business School, where he studies leadership and negotiation. He teaches a popular second-year course on corporate diplomacy, which explores how executives negotiate with other business leaders, government officials, the media, and other stakeholders to shape the external environments of their organizations.

Prior to joining the HBS faculty in 1996, Watkins was an Associate Professor at Harvard's Kennedy School of Government. While at the Kennedy School, he studied complex international diplomacy negotiations in the Middle East, Korea, and the Balkans and coauthored *Breakthrough International Negotiation: How Great Negotiators Transformed the World's Toughest Post–Cold War Conflicts.*

Watkins is also the author of *Breakthrough Business Negotiation: A Toolbox for Managers,* which won the CPR Institute's prize for best book in the field of negotiation in 2002, and coauthor of *Winning the Influence Game: What Every Business Leader Should Know About Government* and *Right from the Start: Taking Charge in a New Leadership Role.*